The short guide to gender

Kath Woodward

D1335066

First published in Great Britain in 2011 by

The Policy Press
University of Bristol
Fourth Floor
Beacon House
Queen's Road
Bristol BS8 1QU
UK

t: +44 (0)117 331 4054
f: +44 (0)117 331 4093
tpp-info@bristol.ac.uk
www.policypress.co.uk

North American office:
The Policy Press
c/o International Specialized Books Services
920 NE 58th Avenue, Suite 300
Portland, OR 97213-3786, USA
t: +1 503 287 3093
f: +1 503 280 8832
info@isbs.com

© The Policy Press 2011

British Library Cataloguing in Publication Data
A catalogue record for this book is available from the British Library.

Library of Congress Cataloging-in-Publication Data
A catalog record for this book has been requested.

ISBN 978 1 84742 763 2 paperback

Cover design by The Policy Press.
Front image kindly supplied by stock.xchng
Printed and bound in Great Britain by TJ International, Padstow.
The Policy Press uses environmentally responsible print partners.

To Reuben

Contents

Acknowledgements		vii
Introduction		ix
one	Putting gender on the agenda	1
two	Sex and gender; sex/gender	21
three	Different and the same?	41
four	Gendered bodies: gendered representations	65
five	Post gender? Does gender still matter?	87
six	Conclusion	107
Glossary		115
References		129

Acknowledgements

I would like to thank Raia Prokhovnik and the Feminist Reading Group at the Open University for such stimulating and useful discussions.

This book also owes a great deal to Sophie Woodward, my co-author of *Why feminism matters* and my daughter. The experience of working on the book together and our cross-generational conversations were so productive, as well as being very enjoyable.

Thanks also to Steve Woodward for doing the index.

Introduction

In a very popular UK comedy series, *Only Fools and Horses*, which started in the 1980s, in one episode one of the main characters becomes a father. He rushes out of the labour ward where his partner has just given birth to their son to greet his brother with the happy news. 'What is it?' asks his brother. 'It's a little baby,' he replies, in a response that elicits loud laughter from the audience. Why is this so funny? We know, of course, that the expected response at this moment is to announce the gender of the infant. It is funny because it is absurd not to realise this. What was the new father expecting? Of course it is a baby, but what everyone wants to know is, is it a girl or a boy?

This is just the start. What happens next makes gender, and babies are born into social worlds that already have rules about what is appropriate and what is not, according to gender. Recognition of the gender of the infant is a key moment in the social marking of identity. Even small babies are expected to wear gender-specific clothing in blue or pink, which still dominates retail babywear outlets. Gender-neutral colours are available for those who wish to rebel or who are perhaps giving a gift prior to the baby's arrival. Clothing may seem to be more closely concerned with femininity and masculinity and what one looks like, but gendered clothing signifies gendered identities that have deep social meanings that are far from superficial and can impact powerfully on life chances. Most parents can find out if their baby is a girl or a boy before birth through ultrasound scanning techniques. In some cases this may be for a much more serious reason than knowing which colour clothes to buy. Pregnancies can be terminated because the foetus is the wrong sex. In many situations and cultures, parents want to select the sex of their child and reject one of what is perceived to be the wrong gender.

Gender matters, from the moment we are born and throughout the lifecourse. How does it matter? Gender offers a relatively secure and stable marker of identity in a world beset by insecurities and uncertainties as well as opportunities and possibilities. Gender is mostly classified according to visible appearance, for example by anatomical, embodied characteristics that mark one sex or the other. Any ambiguities are treated as exceptions, when appeals have to be made to more complex and less immediately accessible sources such as DNA. It is the outward appearance of the body that is the first source of evidence of sex and gender. As Pierre Bourdieu (1984) has argued, the body is the only tangible manifestation of the person and sex and gender are enfleshed characteristics of bodies that are key sources of who we are. As has at times been argued, it may, however, be the case that sex is one thing and gender another, as is explored further in Chapter Two. What, if any, are the distinctions to be drawn between sex and gender? Common sense would suggest that there are differences; sex is what is largely ascertained and classified at birth, mainly by the physical characteristics of the infant and subsequently lived through the sexed body; for example, through the part that a person plays in reproduction. Gender, on the other hand, is the whole set of social and cultural practices that go with being labelled female or male. A study of gender may offer a blurring of boundaries that recognises more complexities and the sex–gender divide may not be quite so clear. In more recent years, social scientists have also preferred to use the term 'gender' and the reasons for these are explained more fully in Chapter Two. What is important is the myriad ways in which sex and gender are invoked and the times and places in the lives of human beings when gender is seen to matter and is the basis for the actions that we are permitted to take and the lives we are allowed to lead; for what we can do and what we cannot.

At different times and in different places, gender matters in different ways. Gender is not just a description, it is also used as a concept that can provide ways of explaining social relations, equalities and inequalities among and between people whose social situations may be very similar or differ greatly. There is some continuity in the idea of gender, in that all human societies have some recognition of differences that are based on gender and these differences are most commonly divided into one of two categories – women or men – although late modernity has seen more acknowledgement of transgender, intersex and more complex ideas about gender.

This guide looks at 'gender' as a key concept that has become increasingly important across a range of disciplines and in interdisciplinary studies as a means of understanding social relations and divisions and at the connections between sex and gender. Developments in the field of gender studies have led to the articulation of a range of dimensions of difference and gender studies have provided the impetus for new ways of thinking about social relations. Historically, there has been a shift from women's studies to gender studies, which is part of the explanatory framework of the guide, but the emphasis is on asking the right questions about what is happening, exploring the evidence and using theories and concepts to address them in ways that make sense of the social world of which gender is an important component.

Chapter One – 'Putting gender on the agenda' – presents an outline of the field and highlights key questions that are addressed in the guide. What is meant by the term 'gender' and how is it used? What sort of evidence is there that supports the claim that gender is a key determinant of inequalities and of social experience? How did 'gender' enter the field as a concept used to explain social divisions? Why does gender matter? This chapter maps out some of the history of the debates and the links between theory and activism, especially in the context of the women's movement and the role that feminisms have played in putting gender on the agenda, politically and in policy making and practice, as well as in developing theories through which to understand and explain gender relations.

Chapter Two – 'Sex and gender; sex/gender' – explores the relationship between sex and gender and some of the links between sex and gender and biology. This chapter uses examples that focus on parenthood and reproduction to illustrate the different meanings given to sex and gender and the ways in which they are used to explain social worlds. Empirical examples relating to parenthood are used to illustrate how the debates are played out. Recent developments in reproductive technologies, for example, have called into question certainties about sex and gender in relation to motherhood. These are examples of areas of experience where gender difference matters and is marked, but can they be recognised without creating inequalities?

Chapter Three – 'Different and the same?' – explores some of the range of social inequalities that encompass differences among women, such as class, ethnicity, race, generation, sexuality and disability as well as differences between women and men. This chapter uses policy examples such as those relating to anti-discriminatory legislation to explore some of the ways in which gender is relevant to debates about equality and difference and what has come to be called 'diversity policies'. One of the big issues in these debates is the question of whether women and men should be treated the same or differently in order to achieve greater equality as an outcome. Are women's gendered life experiences so different from men's that they need positive discrimination as happens in some neoliberal states, although it is illegal in the UK, or at least different treatment to facilitate social equalities? What does a politics of difference mean?

Chapter Four – 'Gendered bodies: gendered representations' – considers the centrality of bodies to debates about gender but how important are embodied differences in shaping gender and does the dualistic female–male categories adequately fit gendered embodiment? Common sense would suggest that the body each of us has is the determinant of our sex, even if gender cultures vary. This chapter looks at the links between enfleshed bodies and how they are represented. Representation of women's bodies has been a major concern of feminist critiques and women's studies. How are women's bodies represented, for example, in popular culture? What are the effects of the sexualisation of women's bodies?

Chapter Five – 'Post gender? Does gender still matter?' – explores changing times, which include increased gender democracy, including equal rights legislation, participation in the workplace as well as global inequalities and the persistence of injustices. Recent developments have taken the form of stressing the fluidity of categories as well as the materiality of global inequalities. How can the concept of 'gender' be invoked to explain some of these tensions? What can gender studies offer to make sense of social change? This chapter outlines some of the debates and offers some critical assessment of how gender has been reconfigured in more recent thinking.

Chapter Six – 'Conclusion' – sums up the key points of definition and argument and evaluates the current state of play in gender studies, by posing some critical questions about how the concept of 'gender' is used and how it relates to other aspects of inequality and difference in the contemporary world and by returning to the main ideas that have been central to gender studies. Gender difference and gender relations do still matter and asking questions that are informed by critiques of gender has practical and political benefits that cannot be underestimated.

1

putting gender on the agenda

Introduction

All societies have had and continue to have some **gender** differentiation and categories of women and men, but these classifications are often either taken for granted or assumed to be biological and therefore not appropriate for cultural and sociological inquiry. The concept of 'gender' has been largely un-interrogated except as a descriptor until relatively recently, when there has been an explosion of texts and theories that aim to situate gender within the wider social, political and economic terrain. How does being labelled female or male shape life experience and are these two categories sufficient? What sort of social processes go into the making of gender? This chapter presents an outline of the field and highlights key questions that are addressed in the guide by suggesting some definitions of gender and presenting sources of evidence about gender relations in the contemporary world. The chapter also maps out some of the history of the debates, such as how gender has been put on the agenda by feminist theorists and activists and has been developed within women's studies and gender studies. The concept of 'gender' now informs a wide range of disciplines and has implications and applications for policy making. Gender is a way of explaining as well as describing social relations.

- What is meant by the term 'gender' and how is it used?
- What sort of evidence is there that supports the claim that gender is a key determinant of inequalities and of social experience?
- Why does gender matter?

■ How did 'gender' enter the field as a concept used to explain social divisions?

Gender: now you see it, now you don't

Gender has been taken for granted in many aspects of social and political life and it is only relatively recently that gender and gender relations have been the subject of scholarly investigation. In sociological texts, gender was either unmentioned or assumed to be something to do with women. Well into the 20th century, the influential work of the 'founding fathers' of the discipline, whose influence extended well beyond sociology, either ignored gender and sexuality or relegated gender to the private spheres of domestic life and personal relations, which were seen as peripheral. The more important social, political and economic forces were seen to operate in the public arenas of production, exchange, politics and governance. Sometimes gender has been synonymous with women as if only women are gendered and men are a neutral, un-gendered norm, defined by other aspects of social life such as **class**, **ethnicity** or other ways of marking a place in the world. The citizen has tended to be seen as a gender-neutral class of person, who nonetheless is modelled on the white, male middle-class standard.

The concept of 'gender' started off as a marker of language. In some languages, nouns, adjectives and pronouns are gendered feminine, masculine or neuter, although translation from one culture to another is not consistent: a word may be masculine in one language and feminine in another. Grammar can be somewhat arbitrary (ships are she in English), but how we use language and the words that are used to attribute gender to a person, office or object reflects and refracts **power** relations.

Language use marks gender, but it has usually been women who are the marked gender, as in the newspaper headlines 'Three people, including a woman, were involved in the accident' or 'Two aid workers and a woman have been kidnapped'. In sport, the football World Cup is the men's competition; it is only gendered when it is the women's game.

Men are actors and poets, whereas the female version is diminished by a suffix: act*ress* or poet*ess*. The gender of a person may either be assumed to be male, as in the use of the third person pronoun in English (as in the writer ... he ...) or if this is a person in charge, everyone in the role is male, as in the 'chairman'; there are doctors and women doctors. Thus, what we say and how we say it both reflects and makes gender relations and attributes gender identities. What underlies this use of gendered language is the power relations that are in play, for example where masculine is the norm and feminine is a deviation. Gender seems to be a somewhat slippery concept though. What do we mean by the term 'gender', beyond its roots in language?

Definitions

What does 'gender' mean and how is the term used? Gender is already there when we arrive in the world. We are born into existing gender frameworks. As I suggested in the Introduction, human societies not only have criteria for deciding whether the new arrival is female or male, but also a set of cultural practices that mark this, including clothing and the reactions of family and friends, who may remark on how little and pretty the infant girl is but raise her male counterpart in the air, commenting on how big and strong he is – a real boy. From the start, different things are expected of girls and boys. The most obvious definition of gender is that it is based on the existence of two different sexes, which play different roles in the **reproduction** of the species, and a set of cultural practices and ways of being that are associated with them.

Classification is not always as straightforward as the female–male binary might suggest, however. Gender always involves bodies, but it is certainly not just about bodies; gender is about bodies that are situated in the social world and are made and remade by social forces as well as anatomy and enfleshed characteristics.

This book draws on social science, gender studies and feminist contributions to the debates, all of which stress the social dimensions of gender.

Gender:

- includes the ways in which different societies at different times deal with embodied differences between people, with a particular focus on the different parts played in reproduction and the sets of practices and social processes that are involved in being labelled female or male;
- is about **difference** and has to acknowledge differences among women and among men and gender difference is more than the dualism of women and men, it includes a range of differences;
- underpins other aspects of society, including sexuality, reproductive processes, production and consumption, paid and unpaid work, power relations and politics;
- involves social practices and cannot be reduced to biology as if biology were an entirely separate, unrelated dimension of being in the world; biology is part of the mix.

Gender denotes an unequal and largely hierarchical division between women and men, which is embedded in social practices and institutions. The concept of 'gender' has been developed to emphasise the social construction of gendered categories of person to encompass different sexualities and different ways of doing gender that are not restricted to women and men. Gender is embodied and lived through everyday interactions and, although it is characterised by the endurance of inequalities such as patriarchy, it is also subject to change and is a fluid concept, which can be negotiated and transformed as well as reinstated.

Looking at the evidence: gender in the world

How can we know what the life experiences that are shaped and influenced by gender are? Often, documentation such as job application forms and bank account application forms require us to tick the 'Female' or 'Male' box or ask for a title that is usually a signifier of gender, such as Ms, Miss, Mrs or Mr. Gender, as defined as female or male, is often a category that is used in the collection of official statistics that are used by governments to map the demographic changes that inform policy decisions. Gender is one of the tools for classifying populations and official statistics are a useful source of evidence. This chapter uses data from Food and Agriculture Organization (FAO) (2011), International Labour Organization (ILO) (2011) and the United Nations (UN) *Human development report*.

Measuring gender inequalities

Evidence of how gender differences inform and shape social relations and experience still largely demonstrates gross inequalities and discrimination against women. So great are the inequities suffered by women across the globe that in July 2010 the UN General Assembly voted to create a new entity to accelerate progress in meeting the needs of women and girls across the globe. The UN *Human development reports* include a category of gender. The last specific gender report was in 1995, but 2010 marked the 10th anniversary of the programme, which provides a comparative index of development across the globe (http://hdr.undp.org/en/). Even if gender is not the main categorising principle, it is apparent that gender remains an important aspect in understanding development and its delays, and the continuity and persistence of gender inequalities. UN evidence presents a plethora of figures on gender inequalities (www.unwomen.org/factsfigures/).

The majority of the world's poor are women, with women who are farmers, migrant workers and those who are older or with disabilities suffering most. Although women produce most of the world's food crops and work on the land, ownership of agricultural land is largely male, according to the Food and Agriculture Organization (FAO,

2011). Forty-one per cent of women now work outside agriculture, but in some parts of the world the figure is only 20% and women's jobs are low paid, low status and vulnerable. Worldwide, women receive lower wages (17% lower) than men, are less likely to be in senior-level positions, of which only one in four is occupied by a woman, and women have less secure employment. The International Labour Organization (ILO, 2011) forecasted that the global economic recession, which started late in 2008, would result in 18.7 million unemployed women. Caring work and unpaid domestic labour remains the realm of women and this has an impact on women's capacity to engage in education, either because of their caring responsibilities or their families' reluctance to devote their limited resources to girls, whose skills may not be valued in monetary terms.

While in some Western liberal democracies such as the UK there is concern about boys' underachievement at school, especially when compared with the much higher achievements of boys over girls at school in the middle of the 20th century, the global situation is one of disadvantaged girls in education. The first decade of the 21st century saw an increase in girls' access to education, with 96 girls to every 100 boys in primary and 95 to every 100 in secondary schools. The number of girls kept out of school has decreased to 53% of the total but in parts of the world, such as North Africa, 66% of those out of school are girls and in the poorest 60% of households a third of all girls are not in school, whereas in the richest 40% the figure is only a tenth. Perhaps most tellingly, two thirds of the world's 776 million illiterate adults are women.

Health is another field of gender inequality. The gap between rich and poor is most marked in maternal health. Maternal mortality is high in developing countries, for example in Malawi and the Central African Republic the maternal mortality rate is 1,100 per 100,000 births whereas in the UK (which is not the lowest) it is seven per 100,000 births. The vast majority of maternal deaths could be prevented, according to UNICEF and the UN. However, it is not the fact that women have the bodies that carry and feed children that is the cause of the ill-health associated with maternity, but rather it is the management of human reproduction and the resources – or lack of resources – that are devoted to this aspect of wellbeing that create these gender inequalities. While it is the management of the capacity for childbearing that makes women vulnerable in some parts of the world, it is also women and girls who are also particularly susceptible to HIV/AIDS. In sub-Saharan Africa, approximately 60% of all adults living with HIV are women. According to UN figures, in several countries young women between the ages of 15 and 24 are as much as three to four times more likely to be infected with HIV than men of the same age. One factor the UN cites in explanation is the lack of access to education and prevention strategies that are available to women. Another factor could be the forced sex and sexual violence that goes with trafficking. In 2006, 79% of the victims of human trafficking were female. This figure is seen as an underestimation by some, for example Kristof and WuDunn (2010) argue that trafficking and forced sex for work operate on such a massive scale that they constitute what they call 'gendercide' in the 21st century.

Violence against women is one of the most significant aspects of global gender inequality noted by the UN and many other bodies. The World Health Organization's (WHO) study of domestic violence in 10 countries, cited in the UN *Human development report*, found that between 15 and 71% of women reported physical or sexual violence by a partner. Over 60 million women and girls have been forced into marriage before the age of 18 and the UN estimates that up to 140 million women and girls worldwide are suffering the consequences of genital cutting or mutilation, with three million such acts being carried out every year. The UN *Human development report* also notes the gendered impact of armed conflict, a set of phenomena that in earlier times had been seen as a male enterprise with predominantly men the victims. Sexual violence as a weapon of war is not new, but it has become systematic and extensive, for example with over 200,000 rapes in the Eastern Democratic Republic of Congo reported since 1996; a figure that the UN believes to be a vast underestimation. There is stigma attached to being a victim of rape within many societies; the raped woman can be held responsible for the attack. Economic recovery plans post conflict remain targeted at men and women and children are again the losers. The UN recognises these gender inequalities and also asserts the role that women are increasingly playing in countering the violence that has been perpetrated, for example women have headed UN peace missions; out of 27 such missions in 2010, women led four and were deputy heads of five.

Women, however, remain grossly underrepresented in government and decision-making bodies. Women held 19.1% of seats in lower chambers of parliament in May 2010 compared with 11.3% in 1995. It may be improving, but just look at the pictures of governing bodies, especially world leaders, in any newspaper, from the government of the **state** to the International Monetary Fund or G10 summits, from the judiciary and the military to sports bodies such as the International Olympic Committee (IOC), the Football Association (FA) or the Fédération Internationale de Football Association (FIFA). When Hilary Clinton stood for President of the US there were jokes in the media about her husband, former President Bill Clinton, who was impeached in office for lying about his affair with a young woman intern, having to join leaders' wives at summit meetings, perhaps for a shopping trip, or to spend some time with the husband of Angela Merkel, the German Chancellor, the only other male spouse.

The UN notes that there are serious limitations to women's full participation in processes of governance due to negative stereotypes, inadequate support including training as well as violence and intimidation against women in public office. The media may be a sector in which more women now work but in the 2010 UN *Human development report* it was found that only 16% of news stories focused specifically on women. The presence of women remains highly sexualised, with discrimination against older women for example as presenters in the visual media; if women are to be seen they have to be young and sexually attractive.

What this kind of evidence demonstrates is that there is still entrenched and powerful inequality perpetrated through gender difference and, as the UN data suggest, change is only possible through first examining the substance and detail of empirical evidence of gender difference and second using gender as a means of understanding these inequalities so that they can be addressed and resolved.

The UN material described above makes gender explicit but it is not always so and gender in official statistics often means women if it is mentioned. Men may be present as 'partners', for example in data on households, or as the majority when women are defined as in a minority, as in government. Men also may be the unstated minority when women are in a majority, as is often the case in health and poverty figures. Even if discussion of gender focuses on women, men and the construction of masculinity are equally implicated, both in the points of connection among people and in the inequalities between genders. Gender differences and gender as an aspect of social relations underpins many aspects of social life in less dramatic ways than the UN data suggest and gender is not always directly invoked.

The following statements are taken from UK *Social trends* report. This research is carried out each year and makes up the official statistics used to trace patterns of change and provide the necessary information for the practices of governance. For example, demographic trends in the birth and death rates, rates of sickness and life expectancy, clearly shape decisions that have to be made about schools, hospitals and welfare services, to mention but three areas of policy. The evidence below is from the 2010 report, which marks its 40th anniversary and charts changes over a 40-year period. Gender is not always explicitly mentioned but, nonetheless, underpins many aspects of change. Consider the five comparisons in the box below. Which of these is about gender and why?

1   In 1971, the proportion of babies born to women aged under 25 in England and Wales was 47 per cent (369,600 live births). In 2008, the proportion of babies born to women aged under 25 in England and Wales was 25 per cent (180,700 live births).

2   In 1970, there were 340,000 first marriages in England and Wales. In 2007, the number of first marriages in England and Wales was 143,000.

3   In 1970/71, there were 621,000 students in the UK in higher education. In 2007/08, there were 2.5 million students in the UK in higher education.

4   In 1974, 26 per cent of men and 13 per cent of women in Great Britain who smoked regularly were classed as heavy smokers. In 2008, 7 per cent of men and 5 per cent of women in Great Britain who smoked regularly were classed as heavy smokers.

5   In 1970, life expectancy at birth for males in the UK was 68.7 years and for females was 75.0 years. In 2008, life expectancy at birth for males in the UK was 77.8 years and for females was 81.9 years.

Source: www.statistics.gov.uk/downloads/theme_social/Social-Trends40/ST40-Press-pack.pdf

In these extracts from the *Social trends* summary data, gender is explicitly invoked in (1), (4) and (5). Point (2) relates to marriage between women and men as the data do not mention civil partnerships, which were legalised in 2004 and fully became law in 2005, but whether marriage, civil partnership or cohabitation, such data demonstrate gendered practices, which have important implications for social relations and welfare. The huge increase in the UK student population noted in point (3) is clearly the result of changes in government higher education policy but gender is not noted, although this period saw significant shifts in the gender balance, such that many more women are now studying at university than was the case previously. Despite media coverage and alarm stories about the educational underachievement of boys and young men, gender may not impact upon higher education policies and thus is not marked here, whereas smoking habits are. The decline in the number of women who smoke is not so great as that of men. It is not clear why gender matters here, except that the data demonstrate social change and the health risk to the babies born to women who smoke. Gender matters in relation to reproduction and costs of healthcare. The increased longevity of people in England and Wales follows earlier trends, with women continuing to live longer than men, but the gap is closing; a trend that has policy implications that may not involve gender, although the causes of the narrowing of the gap between women and men are very likely to be the result of gender. For example, there have been changing patterns of employment, with fewer men employed in heavy manufacturing industry and work such as coalmining with its concomitant health risks, and women's access to healthcare has been improved, although women are now increasingly involved in stressful competitive paid work in the labour market. These few examples are not representative but are indicative of the inclusion of gender as an important dimension of the measurement of population and of demographic change.

How did gender get onto the agenda?

In the brief account that follows, the concept of 'gender' is situated within feminist and gender studies' theories and practices because critical thinking about gender has been inspired by feminist theories and political campaigns from suffrage movements through what was called 'second-wave feminism' to the more recent critiques of **queer theory** emerging from gender studies. Gender has been seen as the realm of biology or not worthy of serious analysis in much of the canon of social and philosophical comment. Psychology has traditions of theoretical accounts of gender difference arising from clinical practice and sociology in the 19th century and well into the 20th century admitted difference but largely either marginalised its importance in public spheres or attributed gendered relations to biological factors. Karl Marx's critique of modes of production largely excluded reproduction, although his colleague Friedrich Engels' (1972) *The origins of the family, private property and the state* provided a productive account of the sexual division of labour based on an explanation of the emergence of monogamous marriage and the advantages to men of the subordination of women's role in reproduction. Engels argued that it was the social and economic organisation of society that led to the devaluing of women and male dominance, rather than the particular reproductive roles of each sex. Emile Durkheim's (1952) functionalist analyses again stressed the consensual arrangement of a separation of women's and men's roles, with women's relegation to caring in the home serving to benefit the whole society. Some of these sociological critiques have been particularly useful, such as Max Weber's (1976 [1905]) notion of patriarchy, which has been extensively developed in feminist critiques. Gender emerged from rational, largely secular debates about social reform, including education and suffrage. It has, however, been feminists who have made the most important contributions to putting gender onto the agenda, starting by revealing inequalities and presenting critiques of male power. Nineteenth- and early 20th-century thinking about gender was mostly concerned with political campaigns for education and suffrage.

Any study of gender owes an enormous debt to the French philosopher Simone de Beauvoir, who famously claimed in her extended study *The second sex* (1989 [1949]) that one is not born a woman but rather becomes a woman. De Beauvoir presented a long and detailed analysis of the ways in which the gender of femininity in particular is historically constructed through social systems, the public discourses of literature, philosophy and art and through everyday practices, intimate relationships and the routines of daily life. De Beauvoir showed how women were psychoanalytically constituted as 'other' in patriarchal culture. She did not deny the actuality of gendered bodies but argued that bodies are themselves subject to social meanings and depend on the whole context of social life.

Anthropological evidence has been cited to demonstrate the diversity of gendered practices across the globe. Margaret Mead's (1950) work showed how particular practices, such as cooking or weaving, when undertaken by men, received higher social value and acclaim than when done by women. Such practices endure in the 21st century. Celebrity chefs and great French gourmets may attribute their skills and taste to their mother's domestic, culinary expertise, but men still dominate the field of well-paid restaurant cooking. The work of anthropologists such as Bronislaw Malinowski is of particular interest to feminists because it was attentive to **sex/gender** and showed that the more conservative universals of Freudian psychoanalysis, such as the Oedipus complex, were not universal at all but particular to specific societies. Feminists of the so-called 'second wave' took up the debate about biology by distinguishing between biological sex and social and cultural gender. For example, the British sociologist and feminist Ann Oakley (1972) importantly pointed out that while sex, as determined by physical characteristics, was rooted in biology, gender involved a set of cultural practices associated with the two sexes in different societies but with no necessary biological determinism of the forms those practices and customs might take. For example, there is no particular anatomical or physiological feature that predisposes women to picking up dirty laundry and operating washing machines (but not designing them). Oakley drew on the work of the US psychiatrist and psychoanalyst Robert Stoller, who had found the distinction between sex and gender useful in dealing with people whose biological sex was not in accord with the gender category to which they had been assigned. People's expression of discomfort at the disjunction between the body they inhabited and its outward manifestations and who they felt they were, led Stoller to make the distinction. Oakley's work was important in pointing out how the apparent certainty of sex had been used to shape a social category – gender – which was subject to change. She argued that sex might be anatomical and corporeal but gender, that is, femininity and masculinity, were cultural and thus fluid and could be changed and reconstructed. Distinguishing between sex and gender served the purpose of raising questions about what was taken for granted about what women do and what men do and especially about the possibilities of change. It also undermined some of the ways in which what men did was more valued than what women did and the hierarchies of gender. There are two different aspects of this debate. The first relates to the extent to which anatomy, physiology and genetic make-up determine what people can do and be and the second concerns why some attributes and activities, when associated with one gender – men – are more valued that those of the other – women.

Sex and gender are, however, clearly linked. In recognition of this, Gayle Rubin (1975) in the US linked feminism and anthropology to develop the idea of a sex/gender system to acknowledge how each society is characterised by a set of practices and systems through which the raw material of human sex and procreation is shaped by human intervention and gender is the socially imposed division of the sexes and thus a social product. What is important about all these discussions is that they made it possible to think about gender as a social, cultural system, which, first, was often unfair and, second, could be changed and modified. Some groups within the women's movement in the late 1970s argued that gender was the root of all social inequalities. For example, Mary Daly (1978) in *Gyn/ecology* developed new ways of critiquing and challenging male dominance or what she called 'malestream thought'. Those who put gender at the centre of their analyses have variously been labelled radical, cultural or more recently materialist feminists. Such approaches are distinctive because gender is not a substructure, subordinate to class for example, but the prime force in shaping life experience and life chances. Gender is always a factor, enmeshed with other **structures** such as class, **race**, ethnicity, generation or disability.

Such approaches, which give primacy to gender and notably women, are clearly also woman-centred feminism. For example, the French feminists Luce Irigaray (1985) and Helen Cixous (1980) pointed to the ways in which gender had been marginalised through women having been written out of history and culture. Each, in different ways, sought to permit women to speak, to write and to be active agents, not merely a category of person that was not man, as psychoanalytic views of gender had claimed. Irigaray argued for a **politics of difference** (see Woodward and Woodward, 2009) that recognised, for example, the importance of mothers and the mother–daughter relationship rather than basing a whole cultural edifice on men, masculinity and the 'law of the father'. In Lacanian psychoanalysis, male dominance is cultural and imposed through language so that it is when a child first learns language and the symbolic systems of culture that they enter into this law and find out that their father is more valued and important than their mother. This claim is counterintuitive and in some ways absurd. Mothers, as the immediate carers of infants, are likely to be the most significant other in the child's early life. Lacan, however, was describing culture that includes the whole value system that is embedded in language and through which the child is introduced to male-dominated society (Lacan, 1977).

The development of feminist thinking about gender has been widely enmeshed with another key concept, notably that of 'patriarchy', which was developed to provide an explanation of some of the inequalities of gender relations and their historical emergence. The law of the father is an aspect of the social structure of patriarchy in which older men have authority over younger men and all men have dominance over women; things male are valued over things female and whatever other aspects of oppression there may be, such as poverty and racism, there are also the forces of patriarchy in play. If gender is social and cultural and can be changed, patriarchy offers some explanation of the endurances of gender divisions and inequality. One of the major debates within the feminisms of the 1970s and 1980s was about the relationship between patriarchy and capitalist modes of production. Many argued that patriarchal relations emerged with the separation of the private arena of the home and capitalist industrialist modes of production, whereas others argued that patriarchy had a much longer historical lineage and predated **capitalism**. Whichever approach you take, gender is still located within and in relation to social, political and economic systems and whether or not it is specific to capitalism, the inequalities of gender divisions have economic effects. Feminist arguments, like those of Veronica Beechey (1979), Christine Delphy (1996), Heidi Hartman (1981) and Sylvia Walby (1990), were unsettling to the mainstream of sociology, where social class had been defined by the labour market position of the male breadwinner. For example, Delphy (1996) argued that the family was the main enemy of women's liberation. Far from being a safe haven and a refuge from the competitive public arena of paid work, as sociologists of the 1950s and 1960s had suggested, for women the home was a workplace and the family the key site of oppression and the main barrier to women's liberation and independence. Feminists analysed in some detail what work women did in households and the contribution of reproduction to production and the segregation of the labour market itself, all of which pointed to gendered inequalities that related to but often cut across class divisions. Such arguments influenced sociological thinking by creating new ways of seeing social systems and reorientated the study of power. Work became not only paid work but also unpaid work and different forms of labour were recognised, including the emotion work and caring work that is so often seen as women's work and consequently undervalued (Hochschild, 1983).

Feminists have used psychoanalysis themselves, as well as challenged it as an oppressive, phallocentric way of thinking and practising. For example, Juliet Mitchell (1974) in *Psychoanalysis and feminism* used Jacques Lacan's ideas to show how capitalism works through a male-dominated culture in which women buy into their own oppression. Male dominance works through **unconscious** forces, which, she argued, need to be recognised in order to challenge and change them. Patriarchy is reproduced through capitalist modes of production and its associated unconscious forces, which are embedded in family structure and the construction of gender relations. Capitalism can only work if women provide and service the workforce.

By focusing on gender, another concept that had been deployed in social and political analyses also came under scrutiny and transformed, namely 'power'. Power can be conceived in top-down hierarchies or as operating more diffusely through the routines and more subtle persuasions of everyday life. Critiques of gender pointed to inequalities in the distribution of power and the women's movement, with its focus on women's experience claimed for its political slogan 'the personal is political' (Woodward and Woodward, 2009). This was not an individualist claim, but one that pointed to the political nature of intimate relations, for example in families, in relation to sexuality and the rights over one's own body. Domestic violence may often be enforced within the private arena of the home but it is a social act that is the product of particular constructions of masculinity that permit the exercise of power over women.

A focus on gender has also put sexuality onto the agenda as a subject for social and political investigation that is strongly linked to political campaigns and what was called the '**identity politics**' of the 1980s, which challenged class-based politics and pointed to the ways in which other forces cut across class divisions, for example those based on sexual identities, disabilities, race and ethnicity.

Differences among women have also been highlighted. Second-wave feminism was criticised for its ethnocentricity in the 1980s and its failure initially to accommodate the diversity and specificities of women's experiences. This included the campaigns of the women's movement. Whereas white, middle-class women might have been struggling to gain full reproductive rights to limit their fertility, for example through access to abortion, many black American and black British women wanted the right to have babies, either by rejecting imposed contraception or through access to in vitro fertilisation (Carby, 1987). Feminist accounts and feminist politics had to take account of the impact of **globalisation** and the **mobilities** of a changing world in order to explore patriarchy as a global phenomenon. By the end of the UN Decade of Women (1975 to 1985), Robin Morgan had written *Sisterhood is global* (1984), a sequel to her earlier anthology, *Sisterhood is powerful* (1970). Women from what has been called the 'Third World', developing countries and diasporic feminists challenged the homogeneous categories of white feminism. For example, Chandra Talpade Mohanty (1988), in *Under Western eyes*, demonstrated how feminist critiques had created a single category of 'third world women' who were seen as illiterate, poor and ignorant in contrast to the educated, modern Western woman who has control over her identity and her own body. Mohanty's work has been very influential in challenging the gendering of imperialism and providing new strategies for solidarity among women (Mohanty, 2003).

Another aspect of the criticisms of the feminisms of the 1970s and early 1980s was its oversimplification of the sex–gender divide. The earlier debates about gender tended to distinguish between sex and gender and to emphasise gender as the socially constructed partner in this pairing. This rather left sex as under-interrogated, as if sex were uncontaminated by social forces and existed in a natural space. Many social commentators prefer the term 'gender' for this reason, but there is more to it and the sex–gender dichotomy has increasingly been challenged, with more emphases on the materialities of sex. One of the first challenges to arise from the problems of the sex–gender binary came from that of biologist Lynda Birke (1986), who argued that biology and sex were not themselves fixed categories. It was not only gender that was socially shaped. Sexed bodies are influenced by nutrition, healthcare and physical regimes such as exercise. Sports science as well as fashion point to the historical transformation of women's bodies in terms of musculature, stature and distribution of fat. Birke's work focused on biological make-up whereas later critiques came from philosophy and branches of the social sciences.

The two most powerful criticisms of second-wave feminism related to its ethnocentricity and lack of acknowledgement of diversity and to its essentialism and over-simplification of gender categories. Critiques of the lack of attention paid to sex also resonated with others who challenged the homogeneity of the category 'woman' by suggesting that such views were essentialist; that is, they reduced all women to a single category, rather as Mohanty (1988) argued that feminism had taken the white, Western norm as its standard. One approach that has addressed both elements is Gayatri Chakravorty Spivak's (1988) particularly powerful work in 'Can the subaltern speak?'. Her most well-known argument relates to her concept of strategic essentialism. Although she argues that categories, notably those of identity politics, which include women in the women's movement, are restricting because they cannot accommodate diversity and, for example the voices of different women across the globe, including those who have been marginalised and excluded, there is a political case for solidarity and for strategic essentialism. For example, there can be combined feminist activism in demonstrating the absence of women on governing bodies and in public life, which acknowledges differences among women, but still makes a strategic case for political action by women.

Judith Butler's (1990, 1993) work has been enormously influential in challenging the boundaries between sex and gender through explaining how sex too is socially constructed and made meaningful through the scientific as well as social discourses that construct it. According to Butler, sex too is acted out routinely through what she calls performativity. We 'do gender' as we 'do' masculinity or femininity so that sex appears to be stable and fixed and it seems to be natural. Butler's prescription for political action is to challenge these everyday, ordinary routines, to cross the boundaries between feminine and masculine and to create transgressive genders. Butler creates fluid possibilities and her argument is well able to accommodate the diversity of gender – and of sex. Challenges to the female–male binary, for example, include those who do not fit neatly into one or other sex and are intersex, as well as those who transgress gender categories such as transvestites and drag artists. Intersex and the challenge to the insistence on a gender binary are explored further in Chapter Two.

Butler's arguments are radical and have been taken on board by activists and theorists although many have been critical (see Lloyd, 2007). Her arguments are very theoretical and sometimes her language is obscure and difficult to follow. The stress on transgression as the main route into resistance to what she calls the heterosexual matrix might seem too marginal itself and to fail to address the concerns of women worldwide, for example as represented in the UN data earlier in this chapter. However, by questioning the fixity of what is taken to be natural and predetermined and by showing how sex too can be reproduced through the iterative actions of what is appropriate for women and for men, Butler raises important questions that have an impact on taken-for-granted assumptions in everyday life and have wider policy implications. Arguments based on the fluidity and contingency of gender categories not only open up the limitations of having only two genders or sexes but also offer a means of exploring how masculinity is socially constructed, rather than fixed. More recently, in the shift from women's studies to gender studies, men and masculinity have been under interrogation and it has become evident that masculinity cannot be assumed and taken for granted either.

Conclusion

- Gender involves social processes through which the categories associated with gender are constructed; what is appropriate for women and what is appropriate for men.
- These social processes have a particular relationship with bodies and embodiment; gender is not all about bodies but neither is gender all about social processes.
- There is substantial evidence of gender inequalities across the globe with, in most cases, women being the underprivileged and most disadvantaged group.
- Exploring how gender works and explaining inequalities involve some suggestions of how to remedy injustices; feminist critiques of gender involve activism as well as explanation.
- By looking at how gender operates socially and politically it is possible to explore some of the complex and diverse ways in which inequalities disadvantage a range of different people and to bring out the shared experiences among people of different genders based on other social systems. Gender is not at the expense of other aspects of inequality.
- The recognition of gender as an explanation of social inequalities reveals its complexities and challenges simple binaries.
- Feminists and the women's movement have done a great deal to put gender onto the agenda not only by providing critical analysis but also through activism and highlighting strategies for change.
- Some views claim that sex and gender are separate but increasingly they are seen as interrelated; some argue that sex too is socially reproduced.
- Different theories provide a focus and ways of deciding what needs to be done to redress inequalities.

2

sex and gender; sex/gender

Introduction

What is the relationship between sex and gender? Are sex and gender two entirely different categories or are they the same? Are sex and gender both linked to biology and if so how? This chapter uses examples to illustrate the different meanings given to sex and gender and the ways in which they are used to explain social worlds. The debate has moved from taken-for-granted ideas about sex being simply a matter of biology and universal, to the separation of sex as being biological and gender as being socially constructed, as Ann Oakley (1972) has argued. More recently, more complex views of the interrelationship between sex and gender and approaches that suggest that sex too might be socially constructed, or at least subject to the influence of social factors, have been developed.

This book is mainly concerned with the social. It is not its purpose to engage with details of the work of biologists or neuroscientists who argue for the biological bases of sex and gender except in so far as the attributes that are classified as female or male, and more especially feminine and masculine, are themselves social categories. For example, when animals such as rats in experiments are described as exhibiting male behaviour that is linked to what are called 'male brains', they may be said to be aggressive, active, adventurous or strong, whereas female behaviour might be described as passive, timid or flirtatious. This means that human-gendered features are given to animals in support of claims that such behaviour is natural. There is slippage between what is biological or genetic and what is social, and these slippages, and in

—

particular what is social about sex and gender, are what this book is about. Being male is more than having a Y chromosome. This chapter explores how useful the sex–gender distinction is in understanding how we live in the world. It also engages with the problems of trying to explain everything by its social construction. What can an understanding of the processes through which gender is experienced lend to making sense of experience?

Making sense of sex and gender

Ways of thinking about the relationship between sex and gender have undergone change over the last 50 years or so in the social sciences. There was a shift, especially due to work in feminist and gender studies, from the assumption that sex is a universal system whereby people are either female or male and gender is about the attributes of femininity and masculinity, to approaches that stressed the distinction between sex as a biological given and gender as a cultural construct, which are therefore subject to change. More recent approaches, as was shown in Chapter One, suggest that sex is a construction and, far from biological, sex determining gender, gender creates sex.

One of the main concerns of feminist and gender studies' theories and activism has been to challenge essentialism with social constructionist approaches (Woodward, 1997). Gender has been theorised as a social division, like those of race, ethnicity or class, where differences among people are tied up with social structures and institutions that create inequalities.

Much of the work of feminism in the 1970s and 1980s was focused on how femininities and masculinities as sex roles were produced, for example through the socialisation of children, media images and representations, including the dominant narratives of popular culture. Gender was seen as how people learned the culturally and historically specific **roles** of being a woman or a man. The processes involved the acquisition of knowledge about gender as a constant, relatively unchanging, universal identity and the clear labelling of gender roles.

Much of the research during this period drew on anthropological evidence and the work of social psychologists, which showed that gender was learned and was culturally specific. The focus of feminists, however, was on the social values placed on the attributes of gender and the inequalities that largely gave more status, as well as more financial reward to that which was associated with men rather than what was connected to women. Domestic labour, childcare and emotion work were all clearly less valued on all counts than the work men did in the public sector of industry and commerce and when women worked in similar jobs to men their contributions were valued less highly. Feminists sought to challenge gender hierarchies by pointing out the inequalities.

Such approaches might, however, seem somewhat simplistic in their stress on the female–male binary and the idea that all women share the same oppression and feminists began to explore more of the details of how gender, far from being the universal category it had been assumed to be, was constituted as a socially constructed product of **patriarchy**. Gender is thus the result of gendered power differences when men as a class have power over women who thus become a subordinate class; gender is the mark of women's subordination rather than its cause. The political message of such views is one that has resonance with Marxist theories of class. In a society that had no social divisions, gender would not exist.

Within feminist and gender studies, however, it was not Marxist but postmodernist approaches that became most influential in understanding sex and gender and it is worth briefly mentioning the work of Judith Butler (1990, 1993) again in this context because it is so radical in its understanding of sex and gender. Butler is closely linked to queer theory, much of which is based on her questioning of the sex–gender dichotomy, her understanding of gender as a performance, her arguments about gender and sexuality and her claim that heterosexuality is an effect of gender. Instead of focusing on mainstream performances of gender, Butler concentrated on drag, when, for example, a person who is 'really' a man, performs as a woman, usually in exaggerated parodic ways. For Butler, there is no real gender that drag impersonates; it is all acting it out to persuade others that you are the gender that you are enacting. Thus, Butler looks at something that seems to be out of the ordinary, even extraordinary, in order to cast light on what is ordinary and everyday. She coins the term '**performativity**' to demonstrate how far it is the performance of gender, how people play the parts of women or of men, which actually creates the gender roles they are playing. Hence, gender is performative in that it brings gender into being through each repetition of gendered acts. This is not like the more usual use of performance where one person who knows what gender they are, plays another. There is no real, constant gender before the performance. One of the first of these iterative acts through which gender is brought into being is at birth when the child is labelled a girl or a boy and is accorded either a pink or a blue blanket.

Butler questions how useful it is to distinguish between sex and gender by arguing that sex is also socially created. The anatomical body reveals very little about sex; what tells us about sex is the set of social and cultural expectations and attributes that go with being called one sex or another. Sex is constructed everyday through social encounters and exchanges, which depend on gender norms that make sense of a person as male or female. It is not just drag artists who are acting out what sex they are, we are all doing it. Butler's queer theory disrupts the sex–gender binary by challenging the stability and truth of what is called 'nature' and the 'natural'. She also links gender to sexuality in her critique of what she calls the 'heterosexual matrix'. Butler extends the idea of **heterosexism** to encompass a wider set of practices. Heterosexuality, like gender, is not a universal given for Butler, but something that has to be made through ongoing repeated performances of gender, which create the illusion of stability and of something that is natural. For Butler, we do sexuality and we do gender.

Butler is not the first to challenge the sex–gender binary and her work has been criticised for its emphasis on more esoteric and marginal gender practices, rather than, for example, the lives of ordinary women across the globe whose problems, as was shown in Chapter One, are not about uncertain gender identities but about deprivation and injustice in their treatment as women. Butler, like other post-modernists and post-structuralists, seem to leave little scope for collective political action if the category 'woman' is unstable and there can be no sense of solidarity among those who identify as women. Butler has been challenged for being too individualist for this reason. She has denied some of these criticisms and many people argue that her contribution to the sex–gender debate and to contemporary feminist and gender studies is genuinely radical and has significant outcomes for understanding how sex and gender work to promote inequalities in ways that can be challenged and changed.

Case studies

This chapter uses case studies, one from the field of human reproduction and the other from sport. Each is an area of life where, first, there are widely and explicitly recognised differences ascribed to women and to men and, second, albeit different areas of experience, bodies matter. Bodies carry particular importance in relation to gender because the body you have is usually the first signifier of the sex to which you are assigned. We, at least initially, decide what sex a baby is and what gender the baby is classified as having by bodily appearance. Bodies are also important because bodies and biology are not necessarily the same. There has been some slippage between bodies and biology in some of the thinking about sex and gender and, for example, body practices, body shape and size have been categorised as biological characteristics, rather than those associated with a particular gender in particular societies. Bodies carry social and cultural meanings and bodies, including brains, change and are transformed through activity and interaction with the world we live in. These are examples of areas of experience where gender differences matter and are marked, but can they be recognised without creating inequalities and how are the gender differences marked? Are the differences about sex or gender or both?

Case study 1: Human reproduction

Man has baby

Periodically, there are stories about men who have given birth. 'Man has baby' is one such shocking headline, which, for example, appeared in *The Times* in 2008, when a transgendered man, Thomas Beattie, was delivered of a child by caesarean section. This child was born in June 2008, and was followed by a second a year later to make an apparently conventional family with his wife Nancy. In August 2010, Beattie gave birth to his third baby. Beattie has legal status as a man, but was born a woman, Tracey Lagondino, who kept her ovaries and uterus but had a double mastectomy to remove her breasts, which are more obvious external signifiers of femininity and, although essential for lactation were not what Beattie called primary female organs necessary for reproduction. After hormone treatment, Beattie also grew a small beard to create a more masculine outward appearance in accordance with a male identity. Beattie's wife had had a hysterectomy and, although she had been born female and always had and continues to have a female identity, she was not in a position to bear children herself.

Beattie's achievements warranted an appearance on *The Oprah Winfrey Show*, a television forum that was renowned for airing social and ethical issues that had some surprise value. Prime-time television provides some space for debate and also, most importantly, validation for identities that might be contested; recognition within the law is one thing and celebrity acceptance another. The elision of celebrity and reality in such programmes does have shock value and but also may challenge conventional assumptions. Or does it reinforce them?

Beattie's is not the only such shock story; other transgendered men have also given birth, although each instance has involved a person born female who has retained their ovaries and uterus. In 2010, another man who was born female also announced his pregnancy (www.huffingtonpost.com/2010/01/26scott-moore-pregnant-man_n_437503.html). In this case, Scott Moore and his husband Thomas, who were both born female and now identify themselves as gay men, went on to have a child 'of their own' by artificial insemination. In the case of Beattie, much was made of the natural delivery of his third baby, although in media coverage there was no mention of vaginal delivery, which is what natural, as opposed to caesarean section, usually means. Either there is a new definition of natural childbirth or this might be too much information, but it does involve the idea of nature as a relevant aspect of gender. Nature and the natural are often invoked in such cases and nature may mean many different things, ranging from biological to usual and normal. Sometimes saying that something is natural is the same as saying it is morally right. Natural does not just mean something happens, it means the speaker thinks it ought to happen.

Comment

What does this case study tell us about, first, the concept of gender, and second, how gender works in the contemporary world? The example of those who are apparently men giving birth to babies poses two big questions with regard to gender, which have resonance not only for how we think about gender differences and gendered identities but also for what sort of policies we need in place to recognise gender differences:

- Are you the sex/gender you say you are?
- What sort of category is gender – is it legal, biological, social?

The first question suggests that people could be the sex/gender they would like to be and that what matters most is the subjective position of the person who is identifying with either a female or a male gender identity. There is an element of this choice and **agency** in the account of Thomas Beattie, who calls himself a man, even though he has a uterus, which would suggest that he is biologically female. He has acted strategically by retaining the necessary female organs so that he can carry a child, but he has made choices about his gender identity and has opted to be classified as male. In this sense, it would appear that in a liberal democracy, such as the US, albeit one in which there are also strongly expressed and enforced reactionary political views, it is possible to make such a choice. It is not simply a matter of whim, of course, because gender matters as a social structure on which social and cultural systems are based.

Those who wish to have their gender reassigned have to comply with a set of processes and to act in particular ways. These processes include the invocation of medical, psychological, social, legal and cultural **discourses**. They usually start with medical contact and culminate with legal recognition at the end of the process.

Recognition in law is a very important aspect of **transgender** identities as it is for transsexuality. There is an increasing number of campaigns directed at the UN to amend its Declaration of Human Rights to include transgendered people. In many parts of the world (including liberal democracies), lesbian, gay, bisexual and transgendered people are persecuted.

This case study demonstrates a mixture of different elements of gender. In the case of someone like Beattie who is classified as male, this mix of elements is particularly complex as, during his pregnancy and at the time of giving birth, he was biologically a woman with the reproductive organs of a woman. It challenges the biological basis of sex, although a man who was born a woman and has a uterus may more accurately be described as transgendered than as a man. Man gives birth has more purchase, especially in the media and popular culture, than transgendered person gives birth. Beattie's life experience has been that of a woman, and radical surgery and hormone treatment cannot create a different life history as man. What this case does illustrate is, first, the possibilities of alternatives to the simple female—male exclusive binary and, second, the possibilities of social change through legal processes, which provide new categories of gender and permit transformations. It is certainly not all about biology, although the biological make-up of the person is one element, as is embodiment. Bodies exist in a social world, however, and are subject to transformation through interaction with social and cultural forces.

In response to the second question, there is the matter of anatomical features that are associated with one sex or another, like having a uterus. Then there is what might be called 'secondary' bodily characteristics. Beattie's hormone treatment enabled him to grow facial hair and the surgical removal of the breasts he had as a woman make him look more like a man. Cultural factors such as clothing and comportment also contribute to the telling signs of gender identity. In an age of androgynous fashion it is not always easy to decide on the gender of a young person at first sight. The legal processes and changes in the law that enable a person to change the gender that they have been assigned at birth are also important factors to consider in looking at what makes a gender identity. The possibilities of the recognition of transgender identities and of the move from being female to male or male to female are becoming recognised in social policies and rights of **citizenship** and embedded in human rights legislation.

This case study has shown:

- There are biological and embodied differences between people that have an impact on gender identities and demonstrate links between sex and gender.
- There are choices and interventions that can be made to change a person's sex; it is not necessarily fixed at birth.
- These interventions do, however, include biochemical and surgical processes, which suggest the importance of the sexed body in relation to gender identity. It is not enough for people who wish to change their gender identity to adopt the outward, cosmetic appearances of the gender with which they identify; bodies are material in the process.
- Sex and gender are not so distinct as they might appear.

Case study 2: A sporting example

This case study is taken from a different social world, although it is still one that has media coverage. In sport, gender is a very important category. Sport is marked by measurement and sport demands certainties; winners and losers, women and men. While in the wider social and cultural terrain there may be ambiguities and, for example, more fluid gender categories, including transgender in sport, regulatory bodies seek to shape and discipline practice and to provide criteria for measurement. When it comes to gender, this is more problematic in sport than in any other field of activity. Sports clubs have been exempted from some of the requirements of sex discrimination legislation in order to acknowledge separate, single-sex competitions. Sports regulatory bodies are reluctant to tolerate any blurring of boundaries and seek scientific testing of categories, which, in the case of sex/gender, mean one of two possibilities. Gender identities in sport are seen as a matter of scientific verification, which appears to mask all the social factors that are implicated. Legal and social changes have made Beattie's case possible and may be indicative of more relaxed attitudes to transgender in some parts of the world. In the academy and in much of popular culture in late modernity, boundaries are blurred and sex as well as gender can be seen as socially constructed and subject to social and cultural inscriptions that shape classification. In sport, there remain claims to very clear definitions of female and male, with competitions being for women or for men. Boxing is classified by weight, and mixed fights are highly contentious. Even in football, mixed games are discouraged after the age of 13 according to FA regulations. The vast majority of sporting competitions are single sex, especially in the case of contact sport and at the highest levels, which highlights the centrality of the body and how embodiment can be classified by gender in sport.

Gender difference in sport is also haunted by the possibilities of unfair practice, which is usually translated as men trying to gain advantage by trying to pass as women, or performance enhancement through pharmaceutical intervention; testosterone can boost performance, especially in some sports. This suggests cheating, although there seems very little acknowledgement of the fluidity of sex/gender and the possibilities of intersex or conditions where people do not conform to rigidly defined, genetic or physical criteria of the discourses of gender testing.

Caster Semenya

The case of the 19-year-old, South African champion athlete Caster Semenya is an excellent example of how the case of an individual can demonstrate wider issues about the relationship between sex and gender. Semenya's gender was called into question in August 2009 at the World Athletics Championship in Berlin, when she won the 800 metres. She was suspended from competitions until a decision could be made about whether or not she was a woman and thus whether she could retain her medal and compete as a woman. Semenya is fast, so fast that other athletes questioned whether she was a woman, leading the International Association of Athletics Federations (IAAF) to instigate gender verification tests, albeit in a procedure that had been leaked before the 800-metre final at the World Athletics Championships in August 2009. The issue received a great deal of media attention, partly because of this leak to the press before an official announcement had been made. Semenya's photograph appeared in media coverage, generating comments about her athletic appearance being 'masculine'. She was also photographed next to the much shorter, more conventionally feminine British athlete Jenny Meadows, who came second in the 800 metres, again reinforcing the contrast between the two women and implying an advantage to the taller, more muscular Semenya.

In May 2010, the IAAF announced that questions surrounding the gender of the South African 800-metre world champion would be resolved by June 2010. The young athlete had to wait for a resolution of a problem that had been hanging over her since in August 2009, until July 2010 when she was at last exonerated of the accusations that she was 'really' a man. The IAAF accepted that she was a woman.

The majority of cases of gender verification in sport involve those competing as women and there have been cases of men attempting to pass as women, for example in the Olympic Games. This means that such cases usually involve a suggestion of cheating and trying to gain unfair advantage.

The debate, especially as manifest in media coverage, invoked expert scientific and medical commentary in its path from claims of unfair practice and descriptions of an athlete with a body variously described as 'manly' and with a 'strikingly musculature physique' to sympathy for defiant resistance to the humiliation of gender verification testing, especially as expressed by the South African sports authorities. Ideas about fair play were invoked with claims that this very fast woman must be a man. There was less coverage of the view that there are global power geometries in play in the subjection of a black South African woman from a poor community to treatment that would not have been given to an athlete from an affluent world power.

In all the debates, there has, however, been heavy dependence on the expert testimony of medical authorities, not only in accessing the certainty of gender identity, but also in treating what may then be seen to be an individual aberration. Such cases are treated as personal and individual troubles with individual solutions, rather than pointing to the social context in which these troubles are experienced and in which gendered identities are forged and understood. One report suggested that ambiguity may be treated by the use of oestrogen, which would increase body fat and, of course, slow her down (*Telegraph Sport*, 6 July 2010).

Comment

Gender testing has a long history in sport, even though compulsory tests were abandoned at the Olympics Games in 1992. Tests have changed from those based on the embodied features that those accorded expert status can see, to DNA and chromosomal tests and the current more complex panoply of procedures that include psychological testing.

The body of the athlete poses problems with regard to conventional readings of masculinity and how far it is a feature of the body one inhabits or how far masculinity and femininity are manifestations of the presentation of the self, either in Goffman's (1959) sense of a role that is played, or to go further, in Butler's (1990, 1993) words, sex as well as gender are performative. The whole thing is socially constructed and there can be no distinctions between sex as biological and gender as socially constructed because the two are inseparable. Either way, performance and appearance are key indicators of gender identity and sporting practice muddies the waters, because loss of body fat, muscle tone and competitive, assertive, even aggressive body practices and comportment all undermine what can be seen as feminine. Such features mean that, especially in media representations of women athletes, there may be claims that they appear masculine, as in the case of Semenya. This presents problems for those who regulate sport. It also raises issues that are the substance of sociological inquiry and suggests some questions. Are gender identities reducible to anatomy or is this confusing flesh and muscle with body practices and what an individual looks like? Could an individual be the gender they say they are and could an individual state with authority what sex/gender they see themselves as being? Gender identities are made and remade through the interconnections between the inner worlds and lived bodies of individuals and the social worlds they live in and are always situated within the wider field of social systems, values and practices.

Much was made of Semenya's physical appearance in the press, based on the assumption that sex determines gender and there are distinct, observable attributes of gender, such as body size, musculature and even facial expression, hair styles and ways of being and carrying oneself outside the sporting arena. All of these things support claims that someone looks masculine so they must be a man. Bodies in sport are shaped by sporting practices and these practices shape sport, but bodies are gendered and women in sport have to negotiate racialised, heterosexist stereotypes. Women athletes may feel compelled to present themselves as conventionally feminine in order to avoid such prejudice because sport is often characterised by stereotypes, for example of heterosexuality and of masculinity. Semenya's raised levels of testosterone may tell us more about what happens to the body of an elite athlete than establishing any certainty about gender categories. Indeed, the IAAF found it so difficult that it took 11 months to decide what Semenya's family had known since her birth and what her own lived experience had told her, namely that she is a woman (www.telegraph.co.uk/sport/othersports/athletics/7873240/Caster-Semenya-given-all-clear-after-gender-test-row.html).

The delay in the IAAF reaching any resolution may suggest some acknowledgement of the complexity of gender identities and the weakness of a distinction based on the categorisation of human beings into only two sexes. Intersex and a range of different forms of development mean that many people, more than we imagine, do not conform neatly to the clear genetic and physical criteria that the regulatory bodies of sport deploy. However, the Semenya case and those of gender verification in general, raise questions about the connections between sport and the wider society. Who are the experts who are called on to resolve matters, in this instance of gender identity, and what measurements and criteria of evaluation will they use? In the case of gender verification, they largely occupy the realm of science and are predominantly medical experts, doctors, geneticists and, as a concession to the lived experience of the individual, psychologists. Psychologists have produced taxonomies of gender, for example Bem's (1976) sex role inventory, which records typically feminine and typically masculine attributes. Bem listed qualities such as anxious, cooperative and intuitive for women and active, arrogant and decisive for men, which clearly reflected expectations and even stereotypes in the US in the

1970s, but is illustrative of how psychologists use social and cultural descriptions of gender types in their own classificatory systems.

Medical science has played a significant role in the search for certainty and fellow competitors, fans and the general public are reassured that Semenya's testosterone levels have been reduced to acceptable levels. These interventions are part of a long history of medical strategies, whether surgical, hormonal or pharmaceutical, whereby deviancy as socially categorised is eliminated and the norm reinstated. It is a fine line between surgical intervention to benefit those who are excluded because they do not conform and those who are forced into conformity because the state of current knowledge cannot accommodate differences and diversity. Deviant figures have been produced through the language of medical science as well as moral discourses as part of regulatory systems that impose particular norms and ways of being and what could be called 'regimes of truth' (Foucault, 1981).

The very term 'gender verification' suggests that we could get at the truth; a single truth unmediated by social, economic, cultural and political factors that make up the assemblage of the embodied self. The coverage of Semenya's case illustrates how troubling gender is in sport. Images draw on stereotypes of what constitutes masculinity and femininity in the current case, as in so many in the past. Women athletes have to reassure us of their femininity, through comportment and appearance, even when they, through the body practices of their sport, necessarily have very different bodies from their female non-sporting counterparts. Men too are caught up in the same gender matrices, as is illustrated by the homophobia that haunts sport. Male athletes may feel compelled to reassure their fans – and their team mates – that they are heterosexual by the constant presence of a heterosexual, preferably conventionally attractive, partner as a spectator and constant presence.

Public debate is always framed by a moral discourse of 'fair play' that invokes the unfair advantage that men who pass as women might gain in sport, but what is most alarming and distressing about these cases is the humiliation that women undergo in being subjected to 'verification' and the public and expert scrutiny that is reserved for women. The drug testing that has largely replaced the genetic testing in the Olympic Games could be carried out without a specifically gendered emphasis. Sport may set its own rules of engagement but these embodied activities remain enmeshed in the systems of power that make sporting troubles social issues. The field of sport is not exclusively a matter of play and of pleasure (and often of pain). Bodies in sport are not reducible to anatomy, or to genetic composition, but are part of a wider set of power relations that are social. Gender is itself a big issue in sport (Woodward, 2009) and is a field that contributes to cultural expectations and identities. Sporting classificatory systems, like sporting heroes and celebrities, are influential forces in the endurance of some inequalities as well as having the capacity to generate social change.

How does this case study address the two questions posed earlier?

■ Are you the sex/gender you say you are?

Again, any such assertion has to be accompanied by compliance with the regulatory framework in which you are operating. It may be the laws of citizenship or it may be the rules of sport, but gender is not just a matter of individuals making claims. It is, however, the modes of verification and what would count as supporting evidence that are the criteria by which gender is defined and through which the links between sex and gender are made. Some things count and others do not, but when these factors are under public scrutiny, for example of sports regulatory bodies and the global media, there are powerful demands for certainty that a simple 'sex is biology, gender is social and cultural' approach cannot explain. In the Semenya case, much was made of her outward appearance in the early reports of the controversy in 2009, which suggested a simplistic belief in the idea that external manifestations of masculinity in terms of distribution of fat, body shape and size must be the direct result of a biological sex that is male. This was only partially challenged by the IAAF's attempts to use expert medical advice that could prove the case one way or the other. It used psychological advice, maybe as a concession to the impact of social forces on gender, but the argument that there are distinctly female and male traits would not subvert the view that sees gender as determined by biological sex in a one-way process; from sex to gender. Drawing on so many sources of expertise does, however, demonstrate the complexity of the relationship between sex and gender and the acknowledgement that (a) there is no simple one-way relationship and (b) there are social meanings given to what may be seen as medical or scientific discourses.

■ What sort of category is gender – is it legal, biological, social?

The field of sport is both distinctive in that it has its own sets of rules and practices and is part of a wider social world. The idea of gender verification has particular meanings in sport but still appeals to the same kinds of expert knowledge that have wider social purchase. Common sense would suggest that there could be clear evidence from visible physical characteristics or a DNA test that could state unequivocally whether someone is a woman or a man. However, it is not only the existence of a far more diverse range of possibilities, including intersex, that is part of a person's biological make-up, but also the match between these embodied possibilities and social and cultural practices and legislative frameworks. One of the arguments in the Semenya case was that, although she did not fit neatly into the category of being a woman, she had lived her life as a woman and her family and friends had always related to her as female. Again, both the relationship between sex and gender is complicated and there are many factors and forces in play, which do not always match up. The law in many parts of the world has changed to recognise transgender but largely, it seems, not intersex or ambiguity. In the first case study in this chapter, a woman had sought intervention to change from being a woman and was able to be classified in law as a man. In the second case study, a woman who was recognised as female at birth, had always lived her life as female and did not want to change, was challenged because of the presence of testosterone and some masculinised characteristics of musculature. Legal recognition of some of the complexities of gender and the interrelationship between sex and gender are all part of the processes through which sex and gender are constructed.

Conclusion

The dichotomy between being female and being male is one of the most powerful and the most taken for granted in human societies. It is taken for granted in that there is limited questioning of the fixity of this binary and strongly enforced. As Raewyn Connell (2009) points out, if gender identity were so certain and so fixed by biology, why are there so many sets of rules and enforcements socially, economically, culturally and politically across the world and throughout history to ensure that people fit into one or other of the categories. Throughout the lifecourse and especially in the socialisation of children, there are strong proscriptions against acting in ways that are appropriate to the other sex. There are highly influential forces in play to persuade people to tow the gender line.

People are not simply the gender they would like to be, although as the example of Thomas Beattie shows in this chapter, there are changes taking place in gender assignment that call into question a simple sex–gender binary. Beattie is legally a man, which might be seen as gender and yet has what are clearly female reproductive organs, which might be sex, but the outcome of the interface between the two is that he is called a man. As both case studies also show, there are pre-existing categories; people are born into a world in which it is mostly assumed that a child is female or male. These pre-existing categories are classified according to a complex set of cultural and social practices as well as anatomical, biochemical and hormonal criteria.

It is difficult to separate sex and gender within this relationship. Gender is a legal and a social identity; for example, the sports regulating bodies, like official government statistics, have two categories. Demonstrating the complexities of these two case studies does not underestimate the predominance of these two categories. The vast majority of people are female or male and women and men have different reproductive roles. The discussion in the chapter does, however, call into question, first, the claim that sex and gender are separate, with sex being immutable and biological, and secondly, the assertion that biology overrides all other dimensions of sex and gender. The relationship between sex and gender is more complex than approaches that suggest a clear-cut distinction claim:

- Gender includes anatomy, biology and social and cultural regulatory forces.
- Arguments that stress the social construction of gender do not have to marginalise biological factors or embodiment.
- Gender is related to biological and anatomical sex in different ways and the influence is two-way; biology has an impact on cultural performances of gender and gender shapes categories of sex.
- Government policies recognise the diversity of gender and the blurring of boundaries between categories and also shape and regulate those categories.

3

different and the same?

Introduction

This chapter takes up some of the issues raised by the discussion of sex and gender in Chapter Two. First, as social and cultural forces are important in the construction of gender, how do these forces relate to other social forces and divisions? Does seeing gender as a social structure mean that people who share a gender identity are a homogeneous group? What about the other differences within the gender group? How strong are the similarities that women or men, as a gender, share? For example, do women have more in common with other women than with men? If they do not, how could gender be the basis of political activism? Also, if everything is socially constructed and hence fluid and changing, how useful is it to hold onto the categories of women and men if there is no fixity? Where does this leave the social movements that have always striven to fight inequality on the grounds that women are a political category and share the experiences of injustice? In this chapter, I focus on what the differences are among women and what an understanding of gender can offer to both explaining what is the same and what is different, but also, most importantly, to suggest how to maintain programmes for political action, policy frameworks and equitable ways of living in the 21st century.

The chapter looks at differences and similarities and picks up on three aspects of gender that were developed in Chapters One and Two:

- the links between understanding how gender works, theories of gender and politics and practices that are part of such theorising;
- the points of connection and the differences among women;
- the interrelationships between personal and social life, and between the intimacies of personal life and relationships and the public arena of paid work and politics, for example as illustrated in the links between sexuality and gender.

These three points are connected because activists in social movements have often highlighted the rights of those who have been denied free expression of their sexuality or whose sexuality has been marginalised or pathologised. Policies to promote and accept diversity recognise a range of different forms of citizenship. Gender studies have put sexual citizenship onto the agenda and promoted its inclusion in discussions of citizenship.

The focus on gender so far in this book has signposted the links between gender and politics, for example the women's movement has worked to eliminate injustices and gender inequalities. Once you start looking at gender as a social structure you start seeing the unequal nature of gender relations as well as all the ways in which people collaborate and support each other. Social movements and campaigns sought to redress inequalities, many of which were based on gender difference. Identity politics, however, also showed that, although gender was important, there was a whole range of different ways in which it mattered and not all women or all men share the same social positions. Women are more likely to experience inequalities than men as a gender but not all women suffer injustice and many men do. Women and men constitute very diverse groups of human beings. Differences include differences among women, for example of class, ethnicity, race, sexuality and disability, as well as differences between women and men. This chapter focuses on how our understanding of gender and gender politics has been transformed by exploring what is different and what is the same among women. There have been changes in the debates about equality and difference and what has come to be called 'diversity policies'.

Chapters One and Two noted the binary nature of many discussions of gender, for example the sex–gender dualism where one is seen as biological and the other social and cultural. The other notable dichotomy is that of female and male. In most situations where gender is on the agenda and we are expected to record gender identity, we are asked to tick a box that states either female or male. Things may not be that clear, as Chapter Two suggested. In the dualism, sex is biological and gender is cultural, but gender includes embodied characteristics, and biological make-up and biology are understood through cultural categories and are influenced by social forces; the exclusive male and female categories have difficulty accommodating transgender and intersex.

A major focus of this chapter is the extent to which not everyone in the category of woman are the same. Talking about differences among women means asking questions about which women one means. Just as traditional, class-based politics have asked questions about men in relation to social class, but not other aspects of being men, such as ethnicity, race, disability and generation, so feminism and the women's movement have had to engage with differences among women, such as those of sexuality, ethnicity, culture, race, location, generation and disability. Ethnicity and race are central to this discussion.

This question about the differences among women is well illustrated by a speech made in 1852 by a black woman, Sojourner Truth, which has been cited within the women's movement and which continues to have resonance albeit within a different globalised context and time:

> That man over there says that women need to be helped into carriages and lifted over ditches and to have the best places ... ain't I a woman? I have ploughed and planted and gathered into barns, and no man could head me ... and ain't I a woman? I could work as much as any man (when I could get it) ... I have born five children and seen most of them sold off into slavery, and when I cried out in grief none but Jesus heard – and ain't I a woman? (cited in Bhavnani and Coulson, 1986, p 83)

Gender identity may be very important but not all women have the same experiences of disadvantage and discrimination as is so powerfully expressed in this quotation; some women are privileged, for example through their class or ethnic position. How much does the shared experience of being a woman override other differences and distinctions? Are these differences enough to undermine gender politics? This is unlikely, given the evidence of gender inequalities across the globe, which were cited in Chapter One. Gender is a crucial concept in explaining social relations and highlighting how masculinities and femininities are made and remade and how these categories can include and exclude people. This is how sameness and difference operate. Importantly, gender is part of the explanation of the persistence of inequalities and gender permits an understanding of differences among people.

This chapter addresses a range of differences and, in light of Chapter Two's exploration of the sex–gender binary, looks at another set of relationships, namely between gender and sexuality. The connections and slippages between gender identity and that of sexuality are fruitful areas of discussion, which link the politics and practice of gender to theories through which it is understood. How are gender and sexuality connected? If you have any experience of diversity politics, for example in promoting social inclusion in sport or the arts, or of equal opportunities, for example in employment policies, such as those that are the concern of human resources departments, you will be aware of the categories of people who are included or of the categories that are used in cases of discrimination or harassment. Many relate to gender and sometimes gender and sexuality elide. One of the ways in which this binary of men and women is being challenged and transformed is through the inclusion of categories such as trans or bisexual or queer, for example in the ways in which people are classified by governmental bodies. These categories often merge gender and sexual identity.

Much of the discussion about sameness and difference that has had an impact on more recent equality legislation in Western neoliberal regimes in late modernity arises from the 'new' social movements of the 1970s and 1980s.

Social movements and identity politics

The social movements that came out of the civil rights activism of the late 1960s and into the 1970s and 1980s challenged some of the traditional theories and practices of politics and highlighted differences among people that were not based only on social class. Race and ethnicity were some of the main aspects of exclusion from public life as well as achievement in education and employment. The labour movement and socialist politics were criticised for failing to accommodate the demands of those who had suffered racism as well as misogyny. Socialist politics in the West had not taken on board the kind of oppression that women were experiencing in the family either. Family life, although a source of mutual support, love and care, was not quite as rosy as some sociologists who wrote about shared conjugal roles and mutuality claimed. Families were a key site for the operation of patriarchal power, with women's free domestic labour, childcare and emotional labour freeing men to engage actively in paid work and public life. The privacy of the family might have offered a safe haven from the competition of the capitalist labour market but it has also been the main site of domestic violence, especially against women. Domestic violence has only recently been recognised as violence in the same way as acts of aggression against the person are in the public arena such as in the street. The women's movement asserted that the personal was political and gay and lesbian rights put sexuality on the political agenda. There is some dispute about whether the women's movement can be called a new social movement (Richardson and Robinson, 2007) but what was then called the women's liberation movement made the demands shown in the box below, which illustrate the main areas of gender discrimination.

Case study

How is difference being constructed here? How far is each demand based on some assumptions about what women and men have in common with their own sex?

- Equal pay
- Equal education and job opportunities
- Free contraception and abortion on demand
- Free 24-hour nurseries
- Financial and legal independence
- An end to all discrimination against lesbians
- A woman's right to define her own sexuality
- Freedom from intimidation by threat or use of violence or sexual coercion regardless of marital status (rape within marriage was not an offence in the UK until 1992 and marital or spousal rape was not recognised in most US states until the 1990s)
- An end to all laws, assumptions and institutions that perpetuate male dominance and men's aggression towards women.

Comment

These demands are largely based on a definition of women as a homogeneous group of people who are different from men; men are named as the source of many of the inequalities that are identified here. The evidence does support the preponderance of male aggression, for example in the form of domestic violence, but there are questions that could be asked about the specific needs of groups of women who are not recognised here. By the end of the 1970s, differences among women, for example on grounds of ethnicity, race, disability and sexuality, were clear; black women, older women and working-class women all argued that the women's movement seemed to be based on the particular identity of white, young, educated, middle-class women and did not sufficiently recognise their interests. The demands of the movement were more specific to this group and did not acknowledge the shared concerns, for example, of working-class women with working-class men or of the women and men who experienced racism and racist violence and exclusion. Even on the matter of reproductive health, while some women might have prioritised access to contraception and abortion on demand, some black, minority ethnic and migrant women and those with special needs were more concerned with the right to have children and to resist an imposed limitation of these rights through the pressured use of hormonal contraceptive injections such as depo-provera.

Making gender politics visible and the critiques and debates that ensued were most productive and led to global recognition of gender inequalities, for example in the UN decade of women 1975-85, which raised women's integration into the development process and provided the impetus for the growth of thousands of women's organisations, political parties and higher education. Women also participated in trades unions, including shared activity with men such as in the miners' strike in the UK in 1984-85, when working-class women fought alongside men to protect their communities and fight the pit closures imposed by the government led by Britain's first female Prime Minister, Margaret Thatcher. Many of the women involved in the women's movement took their commitment and ideas into the academy and the 1980s saw the growth of women's and then gender and queer studies and more recently men's studies. Masculinities increasingly became the focus of scholarly investigation and debate. Thus, the impact of new social movements was to put cultural change onto the agenda for political action as well as the political and economic change that had been stressed by the traditional politics, for example of the labour movement and its politics of redistribution. The women's movement, like other activist social movements, sought to gain public recognition and to put its concerns onto the public agenda. Both sorts of politics involve a critique of power but whereas traditional class-based politics stressed the redistribution of wealth, the new social movements were particularly concerned with the visibility and recognition of social and cultural identities that had been silenced or marginalised. One such category of person in which gender differences were not recognised was the citizen.

Citizenship

Who is a citizen? A citizen is a person with civil, political and social rights under the state. Citizenship rights have been struggled over by those denied them, as current debates about asylum seekers and refugees demonstrate. Citizenship is not simply a legal category of person, although rights in law are crucial to the role; to be a citizen of the state means having rights to safety and protection and rights of residence. In the increasingly mobile globalised world of the 21st century, citizenship is based largely on place of birth but includes the right to live in the state that one has chosen under certain circumstances that are recognised in law, such as those of asylum seekers (Woodward, 2009a). Citizens of the world also have human rights. Such rights, however, are not portable or transferrable, whatever the aspirations of the UN. There are exceptions as is evident in the case of migrants and trafficked people, for example (Gutiérrez-Rodriguez, 2010).

Citizenship has more dimensions than are included in T.H. Marshall's (1964) definition of a citizen as a person who has civil, political and social rights. According to Marshall (1964), civil rights that were guaranteed by the state came first; the law defends the person and the property of the citizen. Next came political rights, which gave the right to participate in public life, for example through voting. Finally, social citizenship provides the right to enjoy a reasonable appropriate standard of living, for example through education and the provision of welfare. Access to welfare systems, such as healthcare, social insurance, unemployment and housing benefits, redresses some of the inequalities that arise in societies based on the capitalist modes of production, but which such economic systems also make possible. Citizenship thus:

- confers rights;
- is based on place of birth and the law;
- encompasses civil, political and social rights;
- includes elements of social justice, for example through welfare systems of insurance and protection of the most vulnerable.

Citizenship may be about human rights but these rights are differently inflected and constituted according to the gender of the citizen. As feminists such as Carole Pateman (1988) and Anne Phillips (1987) have argued, the central dimensions of citizenship, far from being gender neutral, actually construct women and men differently. This is largely because of the social organisation of reproduction. Women have a particular role within the family and in the private sphere of life. The modern state is itself patriarchal, for example systems of taxation, the welfare state and the law all construct women as wives, mothers and workers (often in a part-time capacity rather than entitled to full benefits and on a career trajectory), all of which create women's dependence on men. The patriarchal ideologies of the post-war settlement in which the welfare state was established in the UK still has resonance although there has been a significant shift from the state to the market and the increased privatisation of welfare.

There has to be some social organisation of the rearing of children and women continue to want children and need support through childbearing and childcare. Fathers have a strong investment in their children and increasingly want emotional connections as well as being the main breadwinner in families. Both mothers and fathers want to spend time with their children but demographic changes and the break-up of traditional family life have pointed to some of the weaknesses in the idealised heterosexual family set-up of the 1950s. Patriarchal family organisation both recognises the need for support for childrearing and institutes the dependence of women on men in the nuclear family. Women are given the responsibility for childcare and are thus not able to engage fully in the labour market, are restricted to low-paid or part-time work and often have interrupted working lives leading to reduced benefit entitlements such as pensions, which perpetuates a cycle of dependence and a subordinate status for women. Dependency was, however, written into the post-war welfare state in the UK and into most democratic welfare systems. Patterns of exclusion from the labour market rob individuals of the necessary resources to play a full part in civil society.

The transformations of **neoliberalism** due to changing labour market demands, transforming family structures and gender relations have led to greater autonomy for women and more recognition of the need for change. Contradictions remain, however, and women are still restricted from full participation in civil society not only because they are wives and mothers, but also because the system defines them by these roles. Women who are not mothers are still gendered through the lens of mothering, which attributes to women nurturing skills and characteristics that make them more suitable for lower-paid caring jobs than higher-paid active assertive ones.

Difficulties remain for individuals, families and communities as well as for the wider society in its construction of citizenship in the conflict between private, intimate worlds of family, relationships and childcare and the public worlds of civil society. For example, in relation to gender, it raises questions about how citizenship is gendered and whether gender differences mean that women and men should be treated equally or whether there is a case for differential treatment to recognise gender differences (Woodward and Woodward, 2009). These are the problems and contradictions that gave rise to what has been termed the 'equality and difference' debate.

Equality and difference

It is not surprising that equality has been a key focus of debates about gender and gender activism. Women seized on the language of equality with its association with rights rather than duties and struggled to gain legal rights and political rights to citizenship. This raises questions about how successful campaigns to achieve equality based on rights have been. Equal rights activism has shifted from the rights of suffrage, the removal of legal barriers in the workplace and concessions towards women owning property in their own name. Those who have been excluded and oppressed have fought for the right to vote and for equal rights. However, although these are important rights, the inclusion of the oppressed can leave the structures of oppression intact.

There is little doubt about the evidence of gender inequality. As UN data shows, however, at the end of the 20th century, although women constituted more than half of the world's population and performed nearly two thirds of its work hours, they received only one tenth of the world's income and owned one hundredth of the world's property. The figures for neoliberal democracies are more equitable but, as Chapter One showed, there are still wide discrepancies.

However, recognising inequalities is one thing; knowing how to promote greater equality is another. A commitment to gender equality does not tell us what form that equality should take. Does it mean equality with men and if so which men? Does it mean equal pay for the jobs women do or that women should be able to do all the jobs that men do and be equally represented in all jobs, including those that have been traditionally male? Does it mean equal responsibilities for domestic labour and childcare or better conditions for mothers? Should there be equal parental leave or are there differences that have to be acknowledged and if so how?

The equal treatment of citizens can lead to **social exclusion**. Current debates about Muslim women wearing the *niqab* or Christians wearing a crucifix have all highlighted the dilemmas that were signalled in the Parekh Report (2000) on **multiculturalism** in Britain. The report also included issues of clothing, including Sikh men on construction sites wanting to wear their traditional turban rather than the compulsory safety helmet. Another issue was the case of a woman who was prevented from attending a nursing course because she wanted to wear her traditional dress of *shalvar* and *quemiz* and not the nurse's uniform. Equal treatment in this case meant discrimination as the woman was refused admission. The *niqab* is not a formal requirement of Islam and is debated by scholars but if a woman feels strongly that her religion requires this form of dress it raises questions about the recognition of difference. Should this coverage of the face be permitted only for religious reasons? This could be construed as the recognition of difference or exceptional treatment that is necessarily unequal. Without the special treatment and recognition of difference, women wearing the *niqab* could be excluded from some forms of employment. There are, however, rational criteria of health and safety that can be invoked, although it is a very fine line between such rationality and unfair treatment that denies differences among people.

The response of neoliberal regimes has ranged from exclusion clauses, as in the case of Sikh men and their turbans in the UK, to the imposition of a single rule for all, as in the French government's prohibition of such traditional clothing. What this issue does suggest is that differences among people have to be addressed and the grouping together of black people, women or people with disabilities is unhelpful because there are specific circumstances in which people live, as women. They are not all the same and other aspects of exclusion intersect. Experience is shaped and constructed through, for example, being a woman and having a disability; the dimensions of social exclusion are not mutually exclusive.

There have been criticisms of feminist campaigns, not only because they fail to recognise the multiple dimensions of discrimination and disadvantage and underestimate the impact of, for example, forces such as racism, the power of **disablist** prejudice and the materialities of social class, but also because in the past they might have failed to see the privilege of whiteness. For example, white women may share some of the taken-for-granted advantages of being white and middle class in racialised societies. Nonetheless, as recent sex discrimination cases show, even the most highly educated, class-privileged women who, for example, work in global banking and investment, experience specifically gendered discrimination in the sexualised, male-dominated culture of the sector. Feminists such as Anne Phillips (1987) have argued that equality policies in the workplace only benefit the well off, which is clearly partially true; employment-based benefits such as workplace nurseries and flexible working practices depend on an individual having a job in the first place. However, the problem of negotiating equality, that is, everyone is treated the same, with difference, which allows for specific needs, for example of women to have maternity leave and recognition of pregnancy, childbirth and childcare demands, still creates difficulties. This version of equality and difference sets up another binary; this time between women's rights and needs as mothers and women's rights and needs as workers. To pose the question as women having to opt either for recognition as workers or for special consideration as mothers is yet another false dualism, which focuses on individual agency rather than social analysis. In this binary, children are seen as a personal choice for individuals, rather than an essential part of any society where childcare is also a social responsibility as well as a personal one.

The equality and difference debate identified by feminists in the 1980s still has resonance in the 21st century. So how have neoliberal regimes attempted to deal with the issues of citizenship and resolve the problems of equality and difference? Can citizenship be expanded to accommodate diversity and differences among women and among men and redress some of the dilemmas posed by the contradictions of equality and difference?

Diversity policies: the UK background

Diversity policies in the UK largely derive from the legislation against discrimination, which embeds the notions of inclusion and fair treatment for all in law.

There are currently nine pieces of primary legislation on equality within the UK, with regulations, codes of practice and guidelines supporting them. The equality and diversity legislation currently covers the eight equality and diversity strands:

- age
- carers
- disability
- gender
- human rights
- race
- religion or belief
- sexual orientation.

The Equality Act 2010 brought together nine separate pieces of legislation into one single Act, simplifying the law and strengthening it in important ways to help tackle discrimination and inequality.

The legislation on which the 2010 Act is based is imbued with the language of fair play and justice, highlighting the inequity of existing practices and making it possible to 'put into discourse' (Foucault, 1981, p11) a new language of equality. Legislation has often focused on fair treatment in relation to paid employment, although there has been an extension into access to services as well as the translation of inclusion and equity into the discourse of rights with European Union Directives of 2000 implementing Article 13 of the Human Rights Act (2000/43/EC) and Equal Treatment Directives of 2000 for religion, belief, disability or sexual orientation (2000/78/EC).

In the case of gender, legislation is based largely on the Equal Pay Acts 1970 and 1980; in the case of gender and sexuality, it is based on the Sex Discrimination Act 1975 and the Gender Reassignment Act 2003. The Equality Act 2006 established a single Equality and Human Rights Commission (replacing the three existing commissions). It is unlawful to discriminate in employment on the grounds of sex, marital status or gender reassignment. Legislation includes a positive Gender Equality Duty on public sector bodies to promote equality of opportunity between women and men, and eliminate sex discrimination.

The next three sections look at examples of the impact of diversity, which arise from neoliberal interventions. The first is an example of the promotion of social cohesion through widening participation in sport and the arts through community engagement. The second is in the realm of sexuality and gender, where sexuality has become a key focus of activism and informs the legislative framework for dealing with discrimination. The third relates to age, which has only more recently figured in anti-discrimination policies and practice and which, especially given the demography of ageing, has particular implications in relation to gender.

The impact of diversity policies

Case study

The following extracts are taken from two UK government policy documents, which are concerned with the promotion of diversity. These could be seen as the outcome of the recognition politics of new social movements, which put different groups of people onto the policy agenda, including women. Each of the extracts seeks to promote wider participation in the arts and sport, which is the remit of the UK Department for Media, Culture and Sport as well as a healthier population. Those identified here, recognised as identifiable communities in the language of the new social movements of the 1970s and 1980s, make up the target groups of such policies. Read through these two extracts and think about how gender is constructed here.

More people taking part in sport and physical activity at all levels will bring a number of benefits. The report is clear that there is strong, systematic evidence of a direct link between regular physical activity and improved health for people of all ages.... We must get more people playing sport, across the whole population, focusing on the most economically disadvantaged groups, along with school leavers, women and older people (DCMS and SU, 2002, p 7).

Arts and sport, cultural and recreational activity, can contribute to neighbourhood renewal and make a real difference to health, crime, employment and education in deprived communities (DCMS, 1999, p 5).

Comment

Forty years after sex discrimination legislation, women are named and categorised as a disadvantaged group. Gender is not the only criterion used here. In the first extract, unspecified disadvantaged groups (which probably encompass minority ethnic and racialised people), school leavers and women are named. Generation matters and there is a particular focus on school leavers and older people, many of whom may be women, of course, but it is again only women who are gendered. In the second extract, there is a more explicit focus on economic factors through 'neighbourhood renewal' and the reference to deprived areas. What is noteworthy about this material is that (a) only women are gendered, (b) women, who are likely to make up 50% of the target communities, are classified as a minority group and (c) differences among women are not noted. Presumably, all women are included and given that women will constitute half of the school leavers, half of the disadvantaged groups and demographically over half of the older people, it looks as if a large number of the target group that is underrepresented in sport and the arts and could benefit from more involvement, are women.

Generation is an important component of debates about community and diversity, however, and one that has often been overlooked. While it is generally acknowledged that, in post-industrialised countries such as the UK, there remains a greater proportion of older women than men, the particularities of gender and age have not had much attention except an acknowledgement in life insurance and in health and geriatric care. It is illegal to discriminate on grounds of age and there have been recent changes in relation to the age of retirement, but there are also very strong gender factors in play that relate to culture as well as economic and financial outcomes of pension rights that are part of citizenship.

Sexual citizenship: gender and sexuality

Gender and sexuality are not the same thing but they are closely connected as is evident in the struggles of social movements for women's rights and gay rights. The critiques of **essentialism**, which characterised these social movements, have been challenged by activists who have stressed the centrality of social and cultural forces in the construction of gender and sexuality. Gender and sexuality are not the same but a focus on gender has led to greater interest in sexuality as a site of oppression, for example through homophobia. The interest in sexuality has also arisen from the social constructionism of women's and gender studies. If gender is not simply the social practice of a biologically determined category of sex, heterosexuality can be seen to be socially constructed too and sexuality is not fixed but fluid. Studies of gender (Beechey, 1979; Delphy, 1996) showed that women's oppression was often located within the private realm of the family as wives and mothers and that it was the power relation of patriarchy that created this oppression. One of the ways in which patriarchy operated was through marriage and heterosexual relations, which accorded primacy to men's sexual needs and power over women's bodies to men. Thus, the importance of sexuality in relation to gender is because (a) sexuality is a site of inequalities and injustices, many of which are shared by women on grounds of gender and (b) if gender is practised and made through social interactions, so is sexuality.

Judith Butler's (1990, 1993) work has been particularly important in theorising some of the links between gender and sexuality and in the development of queer theory, which is discussed in more detail, in Chapter Five. Queer theory challenges the ubiquity and dominance of heterosexuality, its norms and regulatory practices. Queer theory is not only critical. It also demonstrates how heterosexuality becomes embedded in society, for example through policies, practices and everyday encounters to make up what Butler calls the 'heterosexual matrix'.

The links between gender and sexuality are partly historical through the development of different ideas in gender studies and also because of the particular importance of heterosexuality and the family as sources of oppression in some feminist theory. In fact, all gender studies theorists have given much more attention to the negative aspects of the family than traditional sociologists and social philosophers. Once the family and heterosexuality are sites of investigation and research, the more negative as well as the positive aspects become clear. Trans also opens up a whole new area in relation to gender. There are people who have one set of embodied characteristics and genetic and biological make-up and perform another set of embodied characteristics; there are others who seek surgical and pharmaceutical interventions to remake their bodies into a new gender. There are also others who do not fit neatly into either the female or male category and have always been intersex but have to espouse one or other gender.

The elision between gender and sexuality is also apparent in anti-discrimination legislation. The LGBTQ (lesbian, gay, bisexual, trans, questioning – or maybe queer in a postmodernist sense) label is frequently seen in policy discussions and is often linked to gender in policy making and in the implementation of diversity policies.

Case study

Civil partnerships

There has been increasing recognition of same-sex relationships across Europe and in Australia, Canada and New Zealand. In the UK, civil partnerships became legal in December 2005. There was considerable media coverage of the first such partnerships and especially the celebrity ones such as Elton John's. These arrangements were controversial, not only on the part of the Christian Right, who felt that such relationships were sinful, a view held by other religions. Feminists also critiqued the replication of patriarchal relationships such as marriage as an institution for the regulation of sexuality. Some civil partnership ceremonies parodied the straight version of marriage as if this ironic performance made the civil partnership a more radical and political version of the institution. The Civil Partnership Act 2004, in transferring the model of monogamous coupledom to same-sex relationships, may not have challenged heterosexual hierarchies of intimacy.

Comment

This case study demonstrates some aspects of the links between gender and sexuality. Civil partnership challenges traditional gender categories that are based on the female–male dualism. In this binary, gender categories are based on opposite sexes who are classified by their role in reproduction, and marriage is traditionally for the regulation of sexual activity and the procreation of children. Legal changes are designed to provide opportunities for those who are outside these traditional dualisms and to embrace diversity. However, while creating opportunities for more diverse categories of sexuality and seeming to upturn gender expectations, critics pointed out that the particular relationship of the civil partnership merely replaced straight marriage, as an institution, with same-sex marriage; the same institution. Gender and sexuality, although they have points of connection, are not the same thing.

There are intersections and there are disjunctions between the different dimensions of social exclusion and between the diverse aspects of social divisions, which gender studies have put on the agenda.

Gender and age

In the UK, the Employment Equality (Age) Regulations 2006 came into force on 1 October 2006 and provided some protection against ageism or discrimination based on age. The law on age discrimination – whether direct or indirect – applies to employees, jobseekers and trainees. It covers the areas of recruitment, terms and conditions, promotions, transfers, training, terminations and retirement. It also prohibits harassment, bullying and victimisation on the grounds of age.

This could include discriminatory acts against young people or indeed people of any age on the grounds of their age; age is not just about being old. A woman might be discriminated against because she is of a childbearing age. They cannot be dismissed because they are pregnant but employers can find reasons for not appointing a young woman who they feel might leave to have a baby. This is not permissible in law but is very difficult to prove. The Regulations provide protection against direct and indirect discrimination, harassment and victimisation in employment and vocational training, which also acknowledge gender difference. For example, women are likely to have an interrupted working life and to have made fewer contributions to their pension funds than men, because of family responsibilities. There are a number of different factors in play and the gendered experiences of ageing have material bases in financial terms and because of the greater longevity of women in most post-industrialist societies the combination of a limited pension fund and a long period of retirement create difficulties for older women. As was argued in Chapter Two, gender is powerfully shaped and constructed by social forces, none more so than when gender and age are studied in combination. The ageing process has embodied and biological dimensions but age too is socially constructed through experience in particular social and cultural circumstances. The issue of age and gender demonstrates the intersection of different social forces and also shows the social and cultural dimensions of those intersections.

The following case study about the problematic UK policy of having mixed-sex wards in NHS hospitals shows how policies and practices are part of wider discourses about age and gender. What are the issues here and what is the relationship between age and gender?

Case study

Mixed-sex wards

Mixed-sex wards have never been very popular and the Labour Party first called for an end to the practice in 1997. The pledge was reiterated in 2001 and 2006. In 2010, the coalition government declared that shared wards in all but accident and emergency and intensive care units would be abolished by the end of that year, such is their unacceptability. Although a commitment has been made, it is frequently beached.

The criticisms of mixed-sex wards have centred on patients' need for privacy and need to maintain their dignity, especially in the case of older women patients who, according to the Royal College of Nursing (2010), want to maintain their modesty.

Comment

There are several factors in play here. Reports are publicised in the media with emotive stories about affronted older women. The frail and elderly may not be a priority for policy makers but media coverage is more about the cultural construction of age and gender. Patients may well be more concerned about the quality of medical care that they receive than with the gender of the occupant of the next bed but the issue does present a worrying disregard for the most vulnerable. Older people, whether female or male, are indeed likely to fall into this category of vulnerability. The media also constructs the most vulnerable, of course, and there is an underlying implication that the co-presence of women and men, even in a hospital setting, carries some kind of sexual threat; women would be vulnerable and men would be sexually active.

What is most interesting about this example is the intersection of cultural constructions of age and gender and the actual practice of policy implementation. Single-sex wards are stated policy but cannot be implemented in practice. Especially at times of economic restraint, policy makers have to prioritise what they do and dealing with the disadvantages of age and gender may not be high on the list of priorities. Neither age nor gender, however, is just a matter of biology and this example shows the social, cultural and economic factors that make up the categories of person in this case.

Conclusion

This chapter has explored some of the ways in which the concept of gender has addressed diversity among people and the points of connection between different forms of social inclusion and exclusion. Gender works with other social forces that position people in the societies in which they live. This happens across time and space; there are different ways in which, for example, gender and race intersect as feminist post-colonial studies have shown by demonstrating the ethnocentricity of much Western feminism of the second wave, which was criticised for failing to take on board differences among women, especially those arising from the legacy of colonialism. Post-colonial feminists gave voice to the concerns and experience of women in the developing world. Feminist arguments about equality and difference and the intersections of different aspects of social relations, such as age, sexuality, ethnicity, race and disability all point to the different ways in which social structures relate to each other.

The focus of the chapter has been differences among women although more recently theorists have turned their attention to what is distinctive about masculinity and at how masculinities are constructed. There are also points of *connection* between women and men, which override differences of gender at particular times and in different places. A focus on gender as a social structure as well as an empirical and embodied fact makes it possible to look at how masculinity is constructed and at how some seemingly gender-neutral categories, such as citizen, are also based on gender assumptions. By starting with femininity as a cultural and social set of practices and showing how femininity is not a biologically determined by-product of having XX chromosomes, it becomes possible to question how masculinity too is constructed through ways of acting and in relation to femininity. A study of gender also raises questions about the adequacy of the two-gender system. Sexuality elides with gender and has become linked, especially in policy making, but they are not exactly the same, as the discussion of equality and difference also shows.

Feminist and gender studies have shown how the citizen has been assumed to be gender neutral but nonetheless the white, middle-class man has been taken as the norm. A focus on gender demonstrates the diversity of citizenship and the importance of cultural rights in a globalised, more fluid world characterised by **diasporic** mobilities, technological and ecological change and cosmopolitanism. Gender differences are important and a focus on gender as part of an explanatory framework allows more specific analysis of differences among people and the policy decisions that could address inequalities.

This chapter has also demonstrated some of the different and specific ways in which social, cultural, economic and political factors shape gender identities.

4
gendered bodies: gendered representations

Introduction

Bodies are central to debates about gender. Each of us has a body, each of us is a body and bodies are key markers of gender. Common sense suggests that the body each of us has is the determinant of our sex, even if gender cultures vary. The most immediate signifiers of gender are physical appearances, such as the size and shape of the body, the way people move and the clothes they wear and how they wear them. Denim may be ubiquitous in late modernity but women and men wear jeans in different ways (Miller and Woodward, 2010). Different societies may perform gender differently, but gender has a close connection with bodily characteristics; what we do with our bodies and how we do what we do are also gendered.

This chapter uses case studies in which the gendered body a person has is central to how she or he lives in the world. The examples illustrate the importance of flesh and blood bodies and of the ways in which bodies are represented and seen by others. We live in our bodies but that experience is influenced by how others see us, and we are influenced by the images of (often highly idealised or sexualised) bodies that we see in the media. Bodies are not just about biology and anatomy, but neither are they just about images and representations. We can intervene and change our bodies, for example through body practices such as sport and training regimes, through cosmetic interventions such as cosmetic surgery, and, in ways which have been highlighted in recent years, through the advances of medical and technical sciences. This chapter uses the example of a disabled athlete who used such technologies and, in a case of medical science, of post menopausal women, well past childbearing, including one aged 66 giving birth to a baby. Childbirth, as was suggested in Chapter Two, might be one of the areas where we would expect the sexed body to be central to what can happen.

Bodies are flesh and blood

Bodies are, of course, material; bodies eat, bleed, feel pleasure and pain, cry and sweat. We are all born and we all die. There are gender differences in the experience of embodiment, many of which are related to reproduction; for example, menstruation, pregnancy, childbirth, lactation and the menopause are all female experiences (the occasional 'man has baby' story notwithstanding). However, all the experiences and processes that flesh is heir to also have social and cultural meanings and values, and are shaped by social forces outside the body too. People's bodies are affected by social processes. For example, they are affected by economic systems, the distribution of food, work, medicine, education, warfare, sexual customs, political responses to climate change and extreme weather – to mention just some of the social elements that have an impact on bodies. Each of these elements is affected by gender. It is not possible to think of gender and the social organisation of gender as the simple outcomes of the properties of bodies. Bodies are born into and grow within particular sets of social circumstances. The social context comes first, but changes and is changed by the embodied selves who inhabit it. There is a co-production between bodies and their social situation.

The actual material of the body is formed through its interaction with the environment; the food we eat or cannot obtain, the exercise we take, the work we do. Even our bones are gendered. Archaeologists are able to ascertain the gender of a skeleton, not only by the size and shape of the bones, but also by their composition. As Anne Fausto-Sterling (2005) argues, the social world that people inhabit, for example in terms of nutrition and lifestyle, is embedded in their bones, with women's bones having a significantly different composition from men's.

This also raises some questions about difference and the ways in which women and men may carry other embodied differences that have only recently been identified. Patriarchal practices and the assumption of a white male norm, not only as the citizen, but also as the standard for human beings, means that some gender differences have been overlooked. It is not only the shape of the pelvis that may distinguish women from men. As sports medicine has recently suggested, knee injuries in women require different treatment from similar problems in male athletes. Women may experience the symptoms of myocardial infarction differently from men; rather than the crushing chest pain and sensation down the left arm that is characteristic of men's experience, women are more likely to feel a more general malaise prior to an attack. The specific characteristics of gendered bodies can be recognised, however, without building a whole social and political edifice that excludes women from public life. The issue is not so much about sex/gender differences, but about how differences are valued or devalued and the social processes that relate to them.

Another aspect of material bodies is how they move and what they do. For example, in the field of sport, gendered body practices have often been attributed to bodily inequalities, such as size, anatomy, muscle power, body mass and stamina, which have often been elided with psychological characteristics such as aggression (Woodward, 2009b). An example would be that the body mass of a prop forward in rugby makes the person more likely play competitively, to override opposition and to tackle positively. Similarly, one of the arguments used against women's boxing is that women are more fragile, less aggressive and vulnerable to damage, particularly to sensitive parts of the upper body, such as breasts. (This may seem a strange argument given the sensitivity of the human brain, which is the target in most professional men's boxing, but it is specifically gendered). Those who argue for the exclusion of women from the more combative sports or argue that women's competitions should not occupy media space because they are less entertaining, unless they are sexualised, than men's, base their claim on women being smaller, weaker and more fragile than men. Aggression, such as positive tackling, is part of a set of body practices, rather than determined by musculature and body mass. Iris Marion Young (2005), in her famous essay 'Throwing like a girl', argued that the assumption that bodies and practice are one needs unpacking. She claimed that girls embody the practices that they acquire. She examined the practices through which women and girls experienced the world through their movements and how they occupied space. The converse of positive aggressive tackling in sport might be taking timid short steps or crossing their legs and folding their arms to occupy the minimum space when sitting down, while men spread their legs to occupy maximum space.

> The young girl acquires many subtle habits of feminine body comportment ... walking like a girl, tilting her head like a girl ... the girl learns actively to hamper her movements ... thus develops bodily timidity that increases with age. In assuming herself to be a girl, she takes herself to be fragile. (Young, 2005, p 43)

This is more than learning to behave in certain ways; these practices become who you are and mind and body are one in this version of gendered embodiment.

These aspects of embodiment show some of the merging of the material body and its social context. How bodies are seen and represented is another key element of the social world. It is partly through representations that we learn what ways of acting are appropriate and desirable. Being in the world includes experiencing how we are seen and how we see others. Representations create images and ways of acting that we might aspire to.

Representing bodies

Bodies cannot be entirely separated from the ways in which they are represented and made visible and the meanings that are given to embodiment. We are constantly presented with images of what is appropriate for men and for women. These images are frequently sexualised, especially for women, although masculinity is catching up and popular culture displays similarly sexualised images of young men, for example as pop stars or sports celebrities. Feminists from the 1970s have been very concerned with how women's bodies are represented and the influence that such images have in shaping gendered bodies. In the second wave of feminism, protests took the form of campaigning against Miss World or Miss America beauty contests as well as deconstructing some of the imagery of popular culture.

Feminists argued that women were always represented through the medium of the male **gaze**. They claimed that whenever you see pictures of attractive women they are always mediated by the male gaze, whatever the gender of the viewer. Hollywood films depict beautiful women who are viewed through men's eyes by women as well as by men. Women, according to this theory, see themselves through men's eyes, even – especially – when looking in the mirror.

Feminist critiques of the objectification and **sexualisation** of women's bodies have informed some of the debates about the causes of eating disorders, especially in young women. The massive media saturation of images of exceptionally lean supermodels sets unattainable and unhealthy standards to which young women may feel compelled to aspire. Similarly and more recently, third-wave feminists have pointed to the exaggerated sexualisation of images of women, which they describe as **pornification** or **pornogrification**. Women's bodies are always coded as sexual to the extent that in many cases representations of women constitute pornography even in the mainstream media where models and pop stars adopt overtly sexual poses. Images include **symbolising** processes which often create sexualised meanings about gender, for example through advertising. Representation includes the words that are used and the interpretations offered of women's activities and their presence. For example, details of women's sexual and intimate lives are often routinely included in any reference to women regardless of the relevance of such information. References to men are more likely to be restricted to the specific context; to a man's job or office rather than to his personal life and relationships or physical appearance. Bodies and body practices make gender as well as reflecting or representing gender.

The work of Michel Foucault (1981), although he did not write explicitly about gender, has been enormously influential in developing an understanding of how bodies are regulated and shaped by social forces. Foucault wrote mainly about male-dominated institutions and the key role played by professional bodies, such as medicine, the law, education and the penal system, in disciplining bodies. In prisons, disciplinary systems might seem more obvious but medicine and psychology and psychiatry regulate and control bodies, and categorise their practices and their features; the hysterical woman of Freudian psychoanalysis, for example, could be construed as a social construct created by the discourse of psychoanalysis.

Sport was not one of Foucault's interests but it provides a rich field for the exploration of how bodies are regulated and gendered by the different routines and practices that create figures such as the successful athlete, the pugilist and the competitive player. Sport is highly gendered in its disciplinary practices. Similarly, the sporting example of the athlete Caster Semenya, discussed in Chapter Two, demonstrates that embodied characteristics of women and men are not unambiguous. A female athlete is very likely to display the muscular body that is associated with masculinity in the world outside sport.

Medicine targets bodies and might be seen as reacting to damaged bodies rather than in any way creating them. Foucault argued that medicine produced rather than simply discovered knowledge and thus medicine creates body types and, in particular for the purpose of this book, gendered bodies. This is a very radical view, which challenges the idea that there is an underlying fundamental truth about sex/gender; either biological, psychological or social. Truth is made through practice and not uncovered and revealed. Medical knowledge not only creates what medical and scientific interventions can do, but also sets the standards for what it is possible to think.

Recent developments in reproductive technologies have created new possibilities for motherhood as a gendered identity. For example, there are new categories of mother: the egg donor who provides the egg, the host mother who carries the foetus to term and the social mother who rears the child are but a few of the possibilities opened up by new technologies. These new discourses about motherhood and practices of reproductive technologies are normative too and also create categories of good mother or deserving mother who is given access to these technologies and the undeserving mother or the non-mother who is not, perhaps on grounds of ethnicity, disability, social status or being classified as deviant in some way. Some women are more privileged in their access to IVF or assisted conception. Reproductive technologies also call into question certainties about sex and gender in relation to motherhood, as we saw in the example used in Chapter Two, which the media presented as 'man has baby'.

This chapter looks at some of the ways in which bodies are important to a discussion of gender and the ways in which gender categories are represented, for example in popular culture and the mass media. These are changing times and technological and scientific advances have made it possible to intervene in the body. The body is also, of course, the target of our own body projects – at the gym or in the health spa. In late modernity, especially in more affluent parts of the world, people are deeply concerned with improving their bodies through sport, cosmetic surgery and a whole range of therapies and enhancements. One of the main sources of the standards to which we aspire is the mass media and the images that bombard us everyday from the television, on the internet, in magazines, films and billboards.

Representing bodies: representing gender

The representation of gendered bodies and gender identities makes up a large part of popular cultural forms, including the advertising of goods and services, which is so central to neoliberal economies and indeed to the profitability of global capital. There has been a shift in emphasis from production to consumption and in most economic systems, such as that of the UK, consumption is crucial to the maintenance of economic stability. Consumption, like the advertisements that go with it, is powerfully gendered. Next time you watch something on commercial television think about who the target audience might be and note what advertisements appear in the break. Apart from specifically children's programmes, a major criterion that distinguishes the advertising will be gender. If it is a sports programme, there are likely to be a large number of advertisements for beer, mainly lager, and cars. Women, especially those who are youthful and sexually attractive, may be used to promote the product but the version of sexualisation will target heterosexual men, who may also be represented in laddish groups. Romantic comedies, 'chick flicks', soap opera and much reality television will usually have advertisements for products such as cosmetics, health goods, the euphemistically named feminine hygiene products, items for babies and children, domestic items including home furnishing and products that women might purchase for men.

Increasingly, the advertising industry deploys irony, self-referential advertisements and in some cases gender identities may be androgynous, as in the famous Calvin Klein promotions, which featured images of young people whose gender was unclear (but nonetheless very fashionable in their slender embodiment). The majority of advertisements are not ambiguous. Although they engage with social change, with the occasional man performing domestic duties (often with boyish incompetence) or a woman in a business suit rushing out of the domestic sphere, gender identities are central and the message of how to perform masculinity or femininity is pretty clear.

Feminists in the 1970s and 1980s critiqued the objectification of women's bodies in popular culture and argued that women were presented as passive objects of the male gaze and not active subjects. This passivity and objectification sometimes extended to scenarios in which housewives reached heights of ecstasy over a new washing powder or household bleach. Women were represented as confined to a passive role as domestic workers and wives, and the critique unfortunately implied that women viewers appeared to be passive dupes to be so duped by the advertisers.

Such analyses were problematic. Women were not just passive viewers of advertisements, women's magazines and soap operas in a state of false consciousness but could also enjoy these aspects of popular culture and use them either for information or entertainment. It is possible to take pleasure in such aspects of popular culture without being deceived. Feminist critics developed more sophisticated analyses that could accommodate the positive as well as the negative aspects of the pleasures of popular culture and suggested a more democratic gaze and the possibilities of a female gaze. Nonetheless, they argued that gender is central to this cultural terrain and popular culture provides a rich source of gendered **identifications** and a lens through which to make sense of gender in the contemporary world. The excess of visualisation of women's bodies can also be seen as responsible for the increased anxiety about their bodies, which so many women experience. These worries range from anxieties about the clothes they wear, through perpetual dieting, to surgical interventions. These anxieties are also being shared by young men as the airbrushed perfection of almost impossible body types proliferate and target men as well as women.

Gender is increasingly sexualised and linked to sexuality in the contemporary proliferation of the visibility of gendered discourses in the public arena. A focus on the empirical actuality of popular culture and the ways in which it is changing and changes those who are part of it has led to a recent concern about how the shift from objectification to sexualisation has accelerated and become what young feminists of the third wave are calling 'pornification' or 'pornogrification'. The 21st century has seen a resurgence of feminist anti-porn activism organising campaigns against the proliferation of pornography in the mainstream of contemporary life. They argue that pornography and the sex industry permeate and influence leisure and intimacy in public spaces and personal relationships, in technology and entertainment through all aspects of consumerism. Ariel Levy (2005) argues that contemporary culture has become a 'raunch culture' in which women are complicit.

The preponderance of pornography in mainstream culture is less contested than the question of whether it could operate in women's interests in any way or whether, as pornification, it is necessarily oppressive. Some feminist commentators even argue that lap dancing, for example, formerly an activity confined to strip clubs for the entertainment of men, has been taken up by young women as an exercise regime and an alternative to working out in the gym. There is not a very strong feminist argument for this, however, and it is difficult to see this appropriation of an activity formerly linked to exploitation and pornography as empowering (Woodward and Woodward, 2009). 'Empowerment' has become a devalued term in these debates. As Levy (2005) argues, the new liberation of lap dancing looks very like the old objectification.

The term 'empowerment' is problematic for a number of reasons. Empowerment is frequently invoked in relation to clothing and appearance. As Sophie Woodward's (2007) ethnographic research shows, the link between appearance and self-valorisation is very strong and women's bodies and what they wear all make up the identity that is presented to the world and how they see themselves. A crucial part of dressing is thinking about how others will see oneself. As G.H. Mead (1934) argued, the self is made up of the 'I', what is inside and how I see myself, and the 'me', that is, how others see me. Women's relationship with their bodies is more complex than the concept of 'objectification' suggests and, as Woodward's research demonstrates, dressing is often a careful act of constructing the self, which women exercise some control over and negotiate. The process of dressing and then of presenting oneself to the world is often described as empowering in the contemporary language of popular culture and by those who claim that looking good, which usually means looking sexy, gives women power over themselves and their situation. The major problem is in the elision of empowerment and looking sexy. A sexually attractive presentation of the self tends to involve overtly sexualised clothing, which is mediated by a particular male gaze and might be the very opposite of empowering; more a compliance with a strongly sexualised norm that could be described as pornified.

Activists are, however, seeking possibilities for resistance and it is interesting that one of the strongest sites for political activism in the 21st century is the internet, which has been adopted by bloggers and campaigning groups who challenge the gendered and sexualised exploitation of current systems of representation. The World Wide

Web has provided space for unregulated, oppressive, pornogrified material but it has also opened up liberatory and democratic spaces for people to resist oppressions such as homophobia, racism, sexism and pornification. The advances of science and technology offer potential for transformations of the representation of gendered bodies through the communication systems of the World Wide Web and the restructuring of material bodies through a whole range of technological interventions. Such progress in the advancement of technological knowledge and practice might transform human reproduction and our understanding of traditional sex and gender roles in the process, enhance bodies and greatly improve the quality of life for many people in what Donna Haraway (1991) has called the 'promise of cyborgs' – a very different sort of body. Are cyborgs the realm of science fiction or might they have something to teach us about what we understand about gendered bodies?

Changing technologies, changing times

The advances in science and technology that Haraway has collectively called 'technoscience' have played a big part in the transformation of bodies and of embodied selves. Technoscience offers much more than superficial changes, whether in healthcare or cosmetic surgery, which is also used by the affluent to offset the effects of ageing in far more radical ways than the use of cosmetics on the surface of the body. Haraway uses the concept of the 'cyborg' to explain and demonstrate some of the possibilities of technoscience and what such advances can offer in breaking down boundaries, including some of the binaries such as nature–culture, sex–gender and men–women. The case study that follows is about the use of such technological advances in sport, which might be the promise of cyborgs. Sport is a highly competitive field, which is marked by divisions both between women and men and between non-disabled and disabled athletes, with a strong emphasis on the capacities of the athletic body, especially that of elite athletes. This example is also one that demonstrates the power of representation in making sense of bodies.

Case study: Oscar Pistorius

Blade-Runner

'Blade-Runner' is the name given to the white South African runner Oscar Pistorius. His story, as played out in the run-up to the Beijing Olympics and Paralympics in 2008, raised some big questions about the role of technologies in enhancing performance in sport and about the relationship between enfleshed bodies and technology. Pistorius' renaming draws on the title of the film *Blade Runner* (Ridley Scott, 1982) and its concerns with the relationship between human and non-human 'replicants', which, or maybe more accurately, who, can be seen as more human than the humans. Pistorius's science fiction epithet, which invokes the excesses and fantasies of science fiction, derives from the fact that the 21-year-old sprinter is a double amputee who lost both legs below the knees when he was a baby and runs on shock-absorbing carbon fibre prosthetics, called 'cheetah blades', which were designed by the Icelandic company Ossur to store and release energy in order to mimic the reaction of the anatomical foot–ankle joint of non-disabled runners. ('Cheetah' refers to the agility and speed of the animal, but sounds unfortunately like cheater.) In 2008, Pistorius won the right to be eligible to compete at the Olympic Games in Beijing. The Court of Arbitration for Sport ruled that Pistorius be allowed to compete against non-disabled athletes. He had competed in two non-disabled athletics meetings in 2007, but the International Association of Athletics Federations (IAAF) ruled in January 2008 that his prosthetics qualified as technical aids, which were banned in IAAF-governed sports because they were seen to afford an unfair advantage to the athlete. In the end, he failed to qualify for the Olympics but ran in the Paralympics

Comment

This case study is resonant of some of the debates raised in Chapter Three about the rules and regulations that are in place to combat discrimination, but which also construct categories of person, for example by gender or disability. Although gender categories are central to sport, as we saw in the case of the athlete Caster Semenya in Chapter Two, gender is not made explicit in this case. This example has much in common with the Semenya case, however. The issue is presented as the classification of disability and how regulatory bodies such as the IAAF can set the boundaries. This case is also about the question of cheating. Are Pistorius' state-of-the-art blades an enhancement too far that enables him to gain an advantage? Pistorius' experience as a competitive athlete challenges the parameters of the natural body, what might be legitimate means of increasing body competences and achievements in sport and how and who judges what we can do and what we cannot.

Disability and non-disability are also gendered. For example, within the field of sport, the dominant discourse is that of competitive, physically competent masculinity. This is part of the culture for practitioners and the other networks that are involved in the wider field of sport, such as spectators, journalists, media pundits, trainers and promoters. Disabled people are usually grouped with women in activities to promote sport; they are the outsiders and not the representatives of hegemonic masculinity (Connell, 1995, 2005), who are the most successful athletes, nor of the more privileged groups of insiders who dominate media coverage of sport. Raewyn Connell's conceptualisation of **hegemonic masculinity** saw heterosexual men as entrenched in a system of patriarchy, although Connell argued that even though they were the main beneficiaries of the system, they could change their oppressive practices. Not all men are the same and some groups may not be part of the dominant masculinity. Hegemonic masculinity is also racialised and ethnicised and these dimensions of social life intersect with others such as disability and sexuality. This model of masculinity is that to which everyone else, however, is expected to aspire – women and men. In order to compete successfully, women too have to buy into this gender identity and this version of masculinity.

This case is haunted by the assumption that disabled athletes are victims and should not compete with non-disabled people; if they do they would be using aids to gain advantage. Athletes observe that they achieve more media coverage and public recognition in the mainstream sport than they do, for example, at the Paralympics. This is why Pistorius sought to compete with non-disabled athletes. Sarah Storey, the Paralympic medallist, received much more media coverage when she competed in the Commonwealth Games in Delhi in October 2010 than she ever had before in the Paralympics, even though she had won two gold medals, three silver medals and a bronze medal for swimming. She did change her sport to cycling but the significant point is that even when there is specific provision made for disabled athletes, they are still competing in an undervalued space. When Blade Runner did eventually compete, in the Paralympics in 2008, there appeared to be even more emphasis on the advantages that might be unfairly gained from technological interventions. Whatever the benefits, just or unjust, that might ensue from accessing the highest-specification technological aids, they cannot be available to everyone. The moral debate is located within the parameters of the economic and the social. While the Paralympics are based on values of courage, determination, inspiration and equality, it could indeed be the last value that is the most problematic, as is illustrated in competitions where some athletes clearly benefit from more advanced technologies than others. For example, in the 100 metres on 8 September 2008, there was a stark contrast between the rudimentary blades of Vanna Kim, a 40-year-old Cambodian who had lost his legs in a landmine in 1989, and the state-of-the-art cheetah blades of Oscar Pistorius.

Pistorius is also white, which may be acknowledged and addressed in post-apartheid South Africa, but whiteness has been under-theorised and its centrality to the operation of power in social relations has not been fully explored. Just as in feminist critiques whiteness is no longer assumed and left without discussion (Ware, 1992), so whiteness in relation to masculinity has to be considered in its specific contexts.

In the case of the South African runner Caster Semenya, the South African sports authorities argued that she had been badly treated by the international media and the IAAF, because she came from an impoverished family in a disadvantaged black community in South Africa. Pistorius' whiteness is also a factor in this case study.

The purpose of this example is to challenge some of the binaries that underpin gender, notably that between nature and culture, and to demonstrate the extent to which social organisation and cultural and ethnical values permeate all aspects of life. This is not to deny the importance of the material body, but how we deal with it, what support we receive and which bodies we value most make this a far from simple nature–cultural dualism. Technoscience is not value free; neither are athletes only defined by their sport. They are also part of a wider cultural terrain of gender. Athletes are not only classified by gender for the events in which they compete, they are also part of a culture of expectations and practices of gender-specific appropriate behaviour.

The next case study also illustrates some of the problematic relationship between bodies and culture, in one of the areas of gendered experience where both body and gender are central. Whatever the shock headlines of the popular press about men having babies, and the extension of childcare to include parenting and the assertion of the rights of fathers, childbirth is an activity that is most powerfully the domain of women and one that centres on women's embodiment. The women who have babies, however, are not usually post menopausal.

Case study

The mother of all differences

In 2005, a 66-year-old woman, Adriana Iliescu, gave birth to a premature girl by caesarean section in Bucharest, Romania, after having had fertility treatment. She is reputedly the oldest woman ever to have had a baby, although there are some accounts of a woman of 70 who had a baby in India in 2010. This was Adriana Iliescu's first baby and she had not been able to have children before. The foetus implanted in her uterus was the product of donor sperm and a donor egg and she had been given hormone treatment prior to the IVF in order to reverse some of the effects of the menopause. The baby girl, Eliza, weighed 1.4 kilos (3 lbs) at birth. Many people questioned the ethics of helping someone in her late sixties to get pregnant and expressed concerns about the care of a child whose mother could well need care herself before the child reached adulthood.

This is not the only such case. There are variants, for example in terms of the genetic links between mother and baby. In 2008, a 61-year-old Japanese surrogate mother gave birth to her own grandchild, using a fertilised egg donated by her daughter. The clinic said that it performed the procedure because the woman's daughter had no uterus, but did not give details on why she had that condition. A British woman in her sixties received fertility treatment in 2009 and raised the same sort of responses in the public arena, with medical staff having to defend their decisions to assist such women in becoming mothers and deal with the expression of anxieties about the ongoing care of the child.

Comment

The phenomenon of the post-menopausal or infertile older mother who delivers a child highlights some big issues about sex and gender and the body. The interventions of technoscience challenge norms and expectations that have been based on biology. For example, babies are born to women in their reproductive years, that is, during the period when they are ovulating. The example of the older mother also raises issues about whether it is ethically right. The idea of 'natural' seems to include what is morally correct. If something is natural it is right and if it is unnatural it contravenes some ethical code. Natural also means usual and the statistically most usual run of things. Women in their sixties giving birth are unusual, so they become the focus of attention in the public arena. In the sea of sexualised images of young women, which makes up the contemporary media, there is also something troubling about post-menopausal women being recognised as sexual at all, let alone being sexually active. While older men can adopt serious roles as news readers and sports commentators, older women are largely absent from television screens.

It is also the case that decisions have to be made about the scarce resources that are deployed in such interventions. Reproductive technologies are often – or many people would argue, always – rationed because they are expensive. However, what informs the criteria on which decisions are made about who should and who should not access them?

New technologies make even childbearing, the most embodied and gendered of human activities, seem disembodied; every stage in the process is managed by forces outside the body and the body seems to be a receptacle. This is further enforced by the visualisation techniques of ultrasound, which are provided for the majority of women in the West. The foetus is represented in its own little world, as if not part of the mother's body in these images.

Much of the debate about whether or not older women should be allowed access to fertility treatment is underpinned by particularly gendered notions of family. Feminists have argued that the family, especially the nuclear family of two heterosexual parents and their offspring, can be restrictive to women. Within the family, women have been responsible for domestic and emotional labour and for childcare and have thus been prevented from playing a full part in public life. Familial ideologies regulate women's sexuality and freedom to shape their own lives. Although in neoliberal democracies there are few if any legal constraints, there are still residues of patriarchal familial ideas, which regulate women's sexuality. The family is both a source of all that is most positive about human relationships and, in particular historic and social contexts, a source of oppression and disadvantage.

Families are constituted through a complex set of relationships and practices, and include family members who are differently located within the family and at different points in the lifecourse. The word 'family' can obscure some of the differences and the inequalities. This is why in the 1970s and 1980s the family became the target of feminist investigation and study. As feminist critics pointed out, the patriarchal family provided strong support for the oppression of women because the family was seen as a private arena, outside the scrutiny of public regulatory bodies. The family was seen to support economic systems of inequality and as a social institution the family was seen as producing women's economic and financial dependence on men. More recently and partly because of the changing demographic of the workforce with the decline of heavy manufacturing industry and the male breadwinner, attention has been turned to the emotional and sexual aspects of the heterosexual couple as the basis of the nuclear family. It is not only because the family has been used to excluding women from the public arena of paid work and public engagement but also because the family has been the site of men's dominance over women, including being the scene of domestic violence, the vast majority of which is exercised by men against women. The familial power relations that justify men's dominance in patriarchy have also been used to justify men's violence. Issues of justice are central to these debates but these are not only ethnical issues: they also have material effects.

The activist strands of feminism have been interested in proposing alternative forms of domestic living that might be more equitable and which recognise the cultural diversity of families. The nuclear family might have been dominant in the post-war settlement in the 1950s, for example in Australia, Europe, New Zealand and the US, but it is neither universal nor fixed. There is a sense in which the 'older mother', who might be the woman who has built her career and postponed childbearing until her late thirties or early forties or the post-menopausal woman who seeks the assistance of technoscience to have a child, is challenging norms and expectations about the family as the location for childbearing and childrearing with its base of the heterosexual couple with clear gender roles. These two sets of mothers are very different, but each has policy implications. The first example of women in their late thirties or early forties constitutes the larger group and presents a challenge to childcare policies and responsibilities as well as creating some concerns about the declining fertility of women as they get older. The second case of women like Adriana Iliescu is framed by ethical debates and about the allocation of resources within health services, for example through costly reproductive technologies such as IVF and the risks of childbirth to the health of the woman having the baby.

These issues illustrate the dilemmas of neoliberal regimes, which, on the one hand, extend to women the advantages of individual choice and autonomy in conducting their own reproductive lives and, on the other, the problem for the state of financing the outcome of women's decisions and of having to take on the support of children that previous regimes had allocated to largely unpaid women within the nuclear family.

Technoscience too generates new questions about fairness, equity and social justice as well as policy-making decisions that impinge on the family and the support for and regulation of family life across the whole society. The apparent certainties of the gendered body are again thrown into some confusion and, in the case of technoscience, it may be that policy makers have not quite caught up with the advances in the field.

Conclusion

This chapter has explored some of the ways in which bodies and embodiment are connected to and influence gender. Bodies are gendered and they are the site of gender differentiation. For example, the visible characteristics of the body are used to determine a person's sex. Even if gender is defined as distinct from biological sex and a cultural set of properties, it is still the case that gender is largely decided by the body and how it is presented. Some of the most strongly gendered identities such as motherhood have powerful corporeal routes (Woodward and Woodward, 2009). Motherhood is particularly embodied because it involves two bodies in one. Bodies clearly matter in relation to gender but the links are not unproblematic, as this chapter has shown.

Gendered bodies exist in a world in which, first, there are strong expectations about the existence of two genders, second, there are strong expectations about what is appropriate behaviour, comportment and practice for each gender and, third, the impact of the social world on the body is increasingly complex and increasingly possible, for example through the advances of technoscience.

The examples that were cited in this chapter involve embodied selves and a focus on bodies in different situations, which draw on media coverage of how these stories were told in the public arena. For example, the comments that the case of the 66-year-old mother evoked tell us a great deal about how motherhood is constructed in contemporary society. Motherhood is clearly an embodied state and carrying a child and giving birth is a corporeal experience, but who is allowed to be a mother and who is seen as a good mother or a bad mother is socially constructed. Age prevents women in their sixties from becoming mothers without some intervention but the decision as to whether they should be allowed those interventions is social and political. Bodies and the society they inhabit are mixed up together.

Representation and how bodies are displayed and presented in the social world are also important in the construction and practice of gender:

■ Bodies are material and enfleshed; they are not blank sheets on which social and cultural forces inscribe gender and sex. Sex–gender is within the body as well as outside it.
■ Bodies exist within social worlds that already exist but which bodies have an impact on; the body and the social world interrelate and cannot be entirely separated, which is another source of evidence for the links between sex and gender.
■ One aspect of the social world is how bodies and embodied selves are represented. These representations are a source of knowledge

about gender and gender roles, and are themselves constitutive of gender.

■ In the contemporary Western world especially, representations, images and discourses of sex and gender have become increasingly sexualised. Women, in particular, are subject to what has been called 'pornogrification', which shows how patriarchal power operates in the field of gender representation.

■ There are some disagreements about how far women have been empowered and what empowerment actually means but, although women are now more present, visibly and audibly, in the field of contemporary cultures, they are still very likely to be represented through the lens of pornification.

5

post gender?
does gender still matter?

Introduction

The big question in this chapter is how important are gender relations in the contemporary world in light of social change. Gender theories have developed more complex ways of understanding sex and gender. There is more gender democracy, including equal rights legislation and participation, in the workplace. There are also massive inequalities and the persistence of injustices across the globe as well as more routine, everyday inequities. Maybe many of the battles of the social movements, especially those of feminist and gay and lesbian rights campaigns, have been won. Recent developments have taken the form of stressing the fluidity of categories as well as the materiality of global inequalities. How can the concept of 'gender' be invoked to explain some of these tensions? What can gender studies offer to make sense of social change? This chapter outlines some of the debates and offers some critical assessment of how gender has been reconfigured in more recent thinking.

This chapter also focuses on social change and how changes take place. The chapter challenges the idea that change is epochal and suggests that there are transformations but also that there are endurances and continuities. Change is often incremental, uneven and small scale, rather than operating on a macro level of one epoch following another, as was argued by most of the grand theorists of modernity.

This chapter uses two case studies to illustrate some of the changes that are taking place and some of the endurances in ways of thinking

—

about gender and to evaluate the relevance of the concept of 'gender' as an explanatory mechanism underpinning the operation of power and social change.

Post feminism? Post gender?

Feminist theories and activism have given high priority to gender and have indeed put gender onto the agenda. Feminists have been keen to highlight the position of women in specific social situations and to point to their absences or marginalisation. For example, in the labour market, empirical evidence on pay shows that women are concentrated in particular, lower-paid jobs and when they reach middle management they are often confronted with a glass ceiling that impedes further advancement (ILO Wage Gap, 2009). The mobilities of globalisation that have involved the migration of workers have often involved the exploitation of women who are more likely to undertake insecure, low-paid, service sector or domestic work, or through trafficking, sex work. Women are also largely absent from the higher echelons of government, big corporations, the judiciary, the professions, the military, the church and most religious bodies. Feminists have also directed attention to categories of person that, while appearing to be gender neutral, are in fact based on the heterosexual, white male norm. 'Gender' has been a key explanatory concept and a necessary empirical focus. The official statistics of governments, quasi-governmental bodies, charities, professional bodies, universities, corporations and employers all now include gender categories in the collection of data, for example on employees, customers, patients and all end users. Such data are required and now even sports bodies and private clubs are required to demonstrate equality in the treatment of their members by providing such data. To qualify for government or grant funding in the UK, it is necessary to comply with the requirements of equality legislation, such as the Equality Act 2010, and to produce evidence of how equality policies are being implemented.

It could be claimed that the battles have been won in relation to gender and that there is no need for feminist activism because such policies have been put in place in most neoliberal regimes.

Women's studies have merged with gender studies in the academy and these are no longer such attractive subject areas in further and higher education where the emphasis of provision, for example in the social sciences, has moved into what are perceived as more vocational areas such as psychology, counselling and criminology. It may be that gender has been mainstreamed and is included in much of the curriculum so that it no longer demands a ring-fenced area of study. Queer studies has blurred the gender boundaries and focused on the margins rather than the centre, the mainstream and certainly not the malestream. Are all of these changes evidence that gender is no longer needed as a subject of inquiry or activism? Is 'gender' no longer such a useful concept for the exploration and understanding of inequalities, injustice and the way the axes of power operate? Could this mean that we are in a post-feminist era?

In order to consider this question in more detail, I would like to identify some of the main areas in which changes might be seen to have taken place in the shift from the ways in which gender (a) was explained and theorised and (b) informed activism, including the governance of equality when it was first put onto the agenda as part of such a programme in the late 1960s and 1970s. Chapter One presented some of the ways in which 'gender' has been developed as a concept, especially within women's and gender studies. The next section summarises some of the particular developments in relation to thinking and acting about equality and attempting to redress inequalities.

From women to gender: the third wave?

What has been called the 'third wave' of feminism has involved an engagement with some of the issues that were identified above and with the transformations that have been taking place in the globalised economy and in contemporary social, cultural and political life. Recent feminists have taken up some of the problems that were identified with earlier approaches and have embraced new technologies. Many of the debates remain very similar, however. For example, are new technologies liberating or restrictive? It depends very much where power lies in access to and the engagement with these technologies. Older debates were about reproductive technologies and whether they could relieve women of the burden of childbearing, in what Shulamith Firestone (1971) called the 'tyranny of childbirth', or whether these technologies remained in the hands of a largely male, elite of obstetricians. Similarly, the World Wide Web is heavily populated by men and masculinity, for example in gaming culture and the prevalence of pornography. Some feminists celebrate the liminality of cyberspace, where the cyborg is neither wholly human nor wholly machine; this is a transgressive, hybrid space where new gender identities can be forged and played out. The internet, however, also permits older and middle-aged men to pass as teenage boys to communicate with and ultimately meet teenage girls in the flesh, offline.

There are continuities and changes in the ways in which gender is played out and understood in a world in which there are demographic and technological changes, some of which are happening faster than the social, cultural and political value systems can accommodate. There are some key points of change and of connection in the study of gender; in how gender can be understood and what an understanding of gender means for activism and governance:

■ Feminism, gender studies and post-colonialism. Criticisms of second-wave feminism as too white and ethnocentric were followed by the development of post-colonial critiques. Feminists contributed to post-colonial studies as a prominent field of study from the 1970s, which addressed some of the unequal relations between European nations and their former colonies and the impact of imperialism. After the Second World War, European dominance declined and by the end of the 20th century the European empires of the past had disintegrated and been partially replaced by what has been called 'US cultural imperialism' as well as 'US military imperialism'. Feminist post-colonial studies focuses on the disintegration of European colonialism by exploring its endurances and by critiquing colonial and post-colonial encounters through a wide range of approaches, including literature and film. Feminist versions of this approach argue for an analysis of gender that includes the specificities of women's experience, including the privileges of whiteness within the aftermath of colonialism and its new configurations. Gayatri Spivak (1988) has argued for a strategic essentialism, which retains some commonality among women for political purposes but recognises differences, especially those of their situation in relation to colonialism and privilege.

■ Sexuality has become an increasingly prominent focus of both gender studies and its incorporation into equality legislation in neoliberal governance. Activists and theorists have pointed to the persistence of homophobia through deconstructions of how heterosexuality has been constantly reinforced as the norm. Queer theory has developed to provide more complex accounts of how gender and sexuality are related, drawing on the work of Judith Butler (1990, 1993). Such approaches challenge the fixity of two gender categories and permit joint activism for men or women on grounds of sexuality. The distinction between gender and sexuality is crucial to queer theory, which concentrates on sexuality rather than gender. Queer theory has been criticised for its complex language, which distances it from the concerns of people outside the academy and its focus on more limited social fields, but it has been very influential, for example in the reshaping of categories within legislation, which now often include LGBTQI (lesbian, gay, bisexual, trans, queer, questioning and intersex).

■ Feminists, pro-feminists and gender theorists and activists have begun to focus on masculinity as a gender category and to show some of the diverse ways in which masculinity too is (a) socially constructed and (b) not an unstated category and synonymous with human being; it is not only women who are gendered. Feminists have developed Raewyn Connell's (1995) work, which showed how masculinities were formed through a relationship between personal lives and social structures. Feminist critics have stressed the changing aspects of masculinity (Woodward, 2007) and argue that hegemonic masculinity is never totally comprehensive; there is always some space for subordinate versions of masculinity as alternative gender identities, which also offer resistance. Masculinities, like femininities, have to encompass marginalised identities based on the exclusions of ethnicity, class, race, disability, religion, sexuality and generation.

■ The liberation of the internet has become (a) an issue of inquiry and debate, for example about the tension between the autonomy and power that the internet offers and its exploitative possibilities and (b) a key space for communication and feminist activism. Cyberspace has opened up all sorts of possibilities for feminist activism and for resistance to stereotyped or restrictive gender roles and sexual identities. If the offline gendered body reinstated gender limitations, the disembodied virtual self was used to challenge traditional binaries as in Donna Haraway's (1991) concept of the 'cyborg'. Web-based activism has also led to a proliferation of websites and the idea and practice of cyberfeminism, like the F word, feminist. com. Cyberspace offers new gender possibilities but not everyone agrees and some critics argue that online gender is just a replication of offline gender.

■ There are consistencies in feminist empirical research and activism, although there has been a shift towards more concentration on sexuality. The private arena of the home and intimate relations is still crucial to gender studies. Domestic violence remains a key issue. Women's Aid in the UK (www.womensaid.org.uk/ domestic_violence_topic.asp?section=0001000100220036&itemT itle=Statistics) presents data that show that one in four women is subject to domestic violence, one incident is reported to the police every minute and, on average, two women a week are killed by a current or former male partner. Men are also subject to attacks: one in six men is the figure given although these figures are based on single incidents, rather than repeated ones as in the case of women, and include minor, that is, not severe and not leading to physical harm, offences. What is relevant about this subject is the recurrent concerns of analyses of gender with the family and the domestic arena and the separation of public and private spheres. This represents some continuity in gender studies and in the activism that seeks to redress such issues.

The academy may have developed a whole new language for explaining gender in the age of cyberspace and shifted from a focus on gender to sexuality and the transgression of boundaries, which may seem to lose altogether the political category of women, and by implication men, but how useful is this? Gender differences and identifying with being a woman or a man remain constant in the routines of everyday life. This raises questions about the extent to which shifting theoretical frameworks and new forms of activism can deal with the continuities of gender as well as the transformations.

Continuities?

The case study that follows is used to address some of the issues about change in this chapter. The case study looks at religion, which is an area that is very often marked by gender and one that has very clear gender boundaries. Religious belief and worship remain enormously important in the contemporary world in spite of claims that the modern world is secular. There may be few states governed by a religious leader but large numbers of people adhere to religious belief systems that base their principles, for example, on the major world religions such as Christianity, Hinduism, Islam, Judaism and Sikhism, which have endured with relatively little change for hundreds if not thousands of years.

Religion and religious worship have their own regulations and customs, for example with regard to gender roles, which are largely respected by the state, although religious intolerance persists in many parts of the world. In neoliberal equality legislation, religion is an area that has been allowed exemptions, for example form employment law, which requires equal opportunities for women and men in accessing all posts. In the sphere of religion, it is permitted to exclude women from high office, for example as priests. There is some controversy about this and change has sometimes arisen after campaigns for equality. In Reform Judaism there are women rabbis, but not in Orthodox Judaism. The Anglican Church has women clergy and the possibility of women attaining the highest office of bishop in the Church of England, although far from being accepted by all Anglicans, is being discussed. However, among Christian churches, the Roman Catholic Church remains firmly opposed to women in the priesthood. The practice of Islam is to have male imams, although there is also discussion within the faith about the possibilities of women leading prayer.

Religious communities and practices offer a fruitful area of discussion about gender in the contemporary world, because religious worship remains a very powerful force across the globe and cannot be seen as a personal and private matter that has no impact on the wider social and political terrain.

Case study

The Pope's visit to Britain, 2010

In September 2010, Pope Benedict XVI visited Britain. He visited England and Scotland for four days in the first ever state visit and only the second visit to Britain since the Reformation. His predecessor Pope John Paul II had visited in 1982 for a six-day tour, which drew huge crowds, but was not classified as a state visit. On this occasion the Pope was invited by the government of England and Wales, where there are an estimated 4.2 million Roman Catholics.

The official itinerary (www.thepapalvisit.org.uk/2010-Visit) started with Pope Benedict being received at the Palace of Holyroodhouse by Her Majesty the Queen. He celebrated a public mass at Bellahouston Park in Glasgow and, in England, made a speech to British civil society at Westminster Hall, met the leaders of other Christian traditions, took part in a service of evening prayers with the Archbishop of Canterbury, led a prayer vigil, met with leaders and people of other faiths and conducted the beatification of the 19th-century theologian and educationalist Cardinal John Henry Newman, who is probably the most famous convert from Anglicanism to Catholicism and a key figure in English Catholicism.

This papal visit was greeted with a great deal of media coverage, but more attention was given in the news and popular media to other aspects of his visit than the events outlined in the official itinerary, which for example did not detail the Pope's audience with survivors of what had been termed 'clerical child abuse'. Pope Benedict spoke to survivors, expressed his concern for what they had suffered and attributed the abuse by Roman Catholic priests to illness. While extending the hand of friendship to the people of Britain, he warned them against what he called 'more aggressive forms of secularism', which had taken over in parts of British society.

The grounds for protests

Opponents of the visit stated that the Pope was opposed to gay and lesbian rights. For example, he opposes same-sex marriage and the adoption of children by same-sex couples.

The Pope has also expressed opposition to abortion, IVF, stem cell research and the use of condoms (not only as contraceptives but also for the purposes of safe sex and protection against HIV).

Some protests were also based on the repeated opposition to the ordination of women in the Catholic Church and Pope Benedict's refusal to countenance any reform. In July 2010, the Vatican reiterated the official view that the ordination of women was a 'grave crime' and on a par with clerical abuse of minors, heresy and schism (www.guardian.co.uk/world/2010/jul/15/vatican-attempted-ordination-women-grave-crime).

Comment

This case study demonstrates the continuing importance of religious beliefs and the resilience of religion in the contemporary world. Thousands of people celebrated the Pope's visit to Britain and he was welcomed by the Queen (who is head of state and head of the Established Church) in what was an historically significant event.

Media coverage downplayed the historical importance, providing limited coverage of Cardinal Newman's contributions to theology and his arguments about the role of personal conscience in ethical actions and decision making and highlighted the recent emergence of details of the scale of clerical abuse in the Roman Catholic Church. The popular media are, of course, more concerned with the need to provide sensational news and to sell papers so it is not surprising that they chose to lead with this story.

However, there are two aspects to this case study that demonstrate how issues of gender are negotiated and represented in the contemporary world.

First, there is the elision between gender and sexuality, which was discussed in Chapter Three. This example covers both. For example, there was protest about the issue of the ordination of women priests. This is overtly about gender as defined by the existence of two sexes and the difference between women and men. This classification is also underpinned by sexuality, based on reproductive capacities and in particular heterosexuality. The gender roles of men and women are shaped by these capacities. One of the reasons why women cannot be ordained as priests is that this is men's role and women's role as mothers is to nurture.

Second, this case study demonstrates changing times and the demand that even the longest established religions have to respond in some way. For example, it is no longer possible to conduct inquiries into child abuse in camera; there has to be some transparency and public assessment of what is happening. Also, demands for change and groups of reformists play a part in the discourses of religion in the contemporary world. Although there are established and embedded belief systems that, for example, proscribe the ordination of women into the priesthood, it is still the case that people organise for change and request reform, because gender roles and relationships are transforming and have indeed changed greatly in the social world outside the belief system. Religion is also part of that world. The last aspect of social change that this example illustrates is the omnipresence of sexuality in the discourses that circulate in the public world. In the world today, sexuality is, in Foucault's (1981) words, extremely voluble. In spite of the official itinerary avoiding any reference to a discussion of sexuality, even in the visit of the Pope, much of the news coverage and political debate is about this very subject. The contemporary world is saturated with sexuality, so it is hardly surprising that there has been a shift of emphasis in gender studies from gender to sexuality and the two clearly have significant points of connection.

This case study is about endurances in constructions of gender, although they have to be negotiated in a climate of change and gender roles and categories. If you look at gender in relation to sexuality, whatever the continuities, this is an area of contemporary life where there have been major shifts in the last 50 years.

The next case study addresses these transformations of gender and is much more obviously about change. In this example, highly educated, well-paid women in the US brought a discrimination case against their employer, the global investment bankers Goldman Sachs. There are a number of relatively highly paid women in banking and city finance, although the sector remains largely a man's world in terms of numbers of employees, especially at the highest levels. The work is extremely demanding in a 24/7 culture of cut-throat competition but change is manifest by the presence of women at all in the sector in posts other than secretarial and junior clerical positions. This is a very competitive world but these successful women have been to the highest-achieving schools and colleges and are now visible, if only on a relatively small scale, in global investment banking.

Legislative changes have also made it possible for women to fight against any discrimination by their employer that they feel is impeding their progress and preventing them from breaking through the 'glass ceiling'. Gender discrimination has been put into discourse, as was shown in Chapter Three, and the employer must take it seriously. However, what counts as discrimination? What sorts of processes are involved in patriarchal constructions of gender – or has the patriarchal power of gender supremacy been replaced by an equal playing field?

Case study

Goldman Sachs discrimination case, 2010

Three women brought a discrimination case against financial services giant Goldman Sachs, claiming that the culture of the firm is testosterone fuelled (www.efinancialnews.com/story/2010-09-16/goldman-sex-bias-lawsuit).

The suit, filed in October 2010, claimed that Goldman Sachs gives its managers, the overwhelming majority of whom are men, unchecked discretion to assign responsibilities, accounts and projects to their subordinates.

The prominent investment bank, of course, disputed the discrimination accusations and claimed that it had made extraordinary efforts to recruit, develop and retain outstanding women professionals. However, the lawsuit attracted particular attention because of the seniority of the women involved. It has prompted an intense debate about glass ceilings and the number of female executives in Wall Street.

The women claimed that managers, whether based on conscious or unexamined bias, most often assigned the most lucrative and promising opportunities, and seats, to men. The suit pointed out that the representation of women gets worse higher up the ranks at Goldman – in 2009, 29% of its vice-presidents were female but women made up only 17% of managing directors, 14% of partners and just four members of a 30-person top management committee.

One of the women, Christina Chen-Oster, who graduated from the prestigious Massachusetts Institute of Technology, had planned a fast-track career in banking. In 1997, she was assaulted by a colleague at work, but failed to say anything for fear of recrimination in the workplace. She claimed that the assault set the scene for eight years of discrimination and blocked opportunity, saying that Goldman discriminated against her on the basis of gender throughout her employment with respect to pay, promotion and other terms and conditions of employment.

She went on to state that her employer also retaliated because she complained of the discrimination. Her argument as reported in the press was that a pattern of discrimination and retaliation began after the senior bond salesman, whose name was redacted in the court papers, sexually assaulted her.

The three women claimed that women at Goldman Sachs are often asked to take on responsibility for training junior employees but are then penalised for diverting their attention away from generating revenues for the firm. They also said that there were specific incidents in which they were discriminated against as women. Chen-Oster, who was paid US$800,000 a year but claimed that her male counterparts earned twice as much, said that a male colleague pinned her against a wall, kissing and groping her after a Goldman-sponsored staff night out at a topless bar. Another claimed she was excluded from golf outings, even though she had played the sport since childhood, and recounted displays of masculinity, including a push-up contest on the trading floor in testosterone-fuelled displays of male bonding. She also asserted that a 2007 Christmas party for a sales team featured female escorts wearing short black skirts, strapless tops and Santa hats.

One of the complainants described how the situation deteriorated after she returned from her second maternity leave in November 2004 to find that Goldman provided her with no meaningful responsibilities or accounts. She was seated with female administrative assistants, despite her vice-president title, and in February 2005 given a downgraded job.

Comment

This case does seem to be about change. These changes take two forms. One is the increased participation of women in the labour market, including at least the beginning of women achieving promotion and working in traditionally male fields such as finance. Related to this is the high educational achievement of young women in many neoliberal democracies. The second point is that the only reason that the case was brought at all is that equality legislation made it possible. There have been significant policy changes in the field of equality and equal opportunities.

There are women, albeit in low numbers, at Goldman Sachs and the women who are there are very privileged if one thinks about women's relative earnings not only globally but in the US.

Gender was explicit in the complainants' statements, but is also explicit within the legislation. Gender was the focus of the argument and of the women's case. It was about unequal gender treatment. The definition of gender that is invoked here is again based on the dualism of men and women and the particularly inequitable nature of this dualism. Gender involves two sexes in a very unequal relationship, but the traditional feminist concept of 'patriarchy' may be too simplistic to explain fully some of the complexities of this version of gender in a changing social world.

The kinds of discrimination that were identified by the plaintiffs in the Goldman Sachs case demonstrate some of the routine practices through which categories of gender and sexuality are made and reinstated. Some of the issues in this case involve routined practices, what Judith Butler (1990) calls the 'iterative practices' that create gender and sexuality. The hegemonic masculinity of a city banking firm could be said to be performative in that this version of masculinity as aggressively heterosexual, asserting men's dominance over women, involves the reiteration of particular masculine practices. For example, men buy the services of 'call girls' and force themselves onto their female colleagues, all actions that bring this accepted masculinity into being. Although the actions are called 'testosterone fuelled' they are not simply the outcome of an excess of this hormone, but these practices are constitutive of the masculinity that is practised and valued in this social situation. Not all men are part of this culture; not even all men in city banking. These are cultural and social practices that are not fixed and determined, but part of the interrelationship between sex and gender, minds and bodies and gender and sexuality.

Equality legislation does increasingly recognise the cultural practices of discrimination and the social and cultural practices that make up gender. This has been seen in the distinction between direct and indirect discrimination, which has been extended in the most recent legislation and the duties it places on employers. For example, in the UK, the Equality Act 2010, some of the key points of which are summarised below, attempts to address problems of the complexity of the processes involved in discrimination. Legislation such as that which has been put in place in the UK also shows the impact of theorising about gender, which emphasises the complexities of relationships and the **intersectionality** of different dimensions of discrimination. Theories of intersectionality have developed to address diverse and wide-ranging aspects of difference but were initiated by arguments about the particular experiences of black women. Patricia Hill Collins (2000) extended earlier critiques and expanded the application of intersectionality in her discussion of black feminist thought to include all women. Although each aspect of inequality is listed in the Equality Act as a separate category, as is shown below, it is the critical analyses of different aspects of inequality that have demanded the recognition of the multifaceted nature of social exclusion.

Equality in the 21st century

UK Equality Act 2010

The protected characteristics listed in the Act are:

- age
- disability
- gender reassignment
- marriage and civil partnership
- race (including ethnic origin, national origin, visible difference, nationality)
- religion or belief
- sex
- sexual orientation.

The Equality Act was designed to harmonise the fragmented discrimination legislation and introduce some new restrictions for employers, many of which suggest discrimination by association rather than direct discrimination, which is based on perception and association. The Act expanded the idea of **indirect discrimination**, which covers circumstances where someone is actually put at a disadvantage but also where they would be put at a disadvantage, for example someone might be deterred from applying for a post.

Harassment covers treatment based on perception and association. Employers are liable if they fail to take reasonably practicable steps to prevent a third party from harassing an individual in circumstances where they have been harassed on two previous occasions.

Discrimination arising from disability is a new aspect of the equality legisation. This occurs if A treats B unfavourably because of something arising in consequence of B's disability. For example, if B is dismissed because of absences arising from a disability, A will have discriminated against B unless the dismissal can be justified objectively.

Questions in pre-employment questionnaires about health can be asked, but an employer cannot discriminate against the way an individual responds to the answers.

Questions can also be asked, for example, to establish whether a disabled person would be able to carry out an intrinsic function of the work concerned or for monitoring diversity.

Equal pay remains a central concern. For example, a claim for equal pay can be made in the absence of a comparator under the remit of direct sex discrimination where the treatment can be shown to be because of a person's sex, such as an employer explicitly paying more to a man than a woman.

Secrecy clauses mean that any provision preventing an employee discussing pay to establish whether they have been discriminated against will be void and that same employee would be protected from victimisation because they have discussed pay.

These different ways of signalling sources of social exclusion and marginalisation represent acknowledgement of the complexities that are involved and in which gender is widely implicated. However, their presence on the statute book is not necessarily any guarantee that the issues will be addressed or that the outcomes of such legislation will mean greater equality (or social cohesion). What is relevant to the discussion in this book is the ways in which gender studies has informed some of these shifts and influenced policy making. Approaches that point to the complicated ways in which different axes of power intersect and show the points of connection as well as the disjunctions, far from being removed from everyday life, have had important political outcomes. Intersectionality can offer rich descriptions of the range of these dimensions of difference. However, it is also necessary to explain imbalances of power and to look in some detail at the temporal and spatial dimensions of inequality. Gender theories are closely liked to explanatory concepts such as 'patriarchy', which do locate power. There is a danger that merely outlining or listing the different dimensions cannot attribute a source to power. Also, in the more diffuse interpretations of the operation of power, for example as experienced in routine everyday exchanges as well as in the regulatory practices of the state, power may be present in so many micro-level encounters that in being everywhere it is nowhere.

Conclusion

Gender remains a powerful presence in the 21st century, which is highlighted by the persistence of gender inequalities as well as the universal importance of gender as part of social relations. There are powerful endurances in gender differences and in dualistic classifications of gender. The definition suggested at the start of this book included the centrality of an understanding of gender that is based on two sexes and this chapter on change demonstrates that this clearly has enormous purchase in the contemporary world. What recent developments in gender theory and in the activism that is based on such understandings of the complexity of gender categories show is that, first, the situation is more complex than a simple binary and, second, sometimes, by looking at the periphery and the margins, it is possible to understand more about the centre and the mainstream.

The discussion in this chapter shows that there remain instances of gender discrimination, even within the most affluent and privileged communities. 'Gender' still provides a useful concept for exploring the operation of power relations at different levels.

Power works in different ways. Power can be coercive and involve force or it can be a whole set of everyday practices. It may be embedded in tradition, explicit and direct; power can be top down and involve institutional backing. Power can also operate diffusely and it may be difficult to identify where it is. In the case of gender discrimination, the idea of indirect discrimination includes a whole set of discriminatory acts, which together make up a culture of unequal treatment. Foucault's (1981) analysis of power has been very influential in postmodernist critiques. The idea that power can work cumulatively through everyday exchanges and in micro level ways is very productive in exploring how gender works.

One of the more recent trends in understanding gender has involved examining some of the links between sexuality and gender and, indeed, in the case of some thinkers of suggesting that the two are interchangeable. There are distinctions between gender and sexuality and there are still cases where 'gender' is more useful as an explanatory concept, but looking at the links is useful in understanding the different ways in which gender identities are reproduced and enacted.

The recent focus on sexuality in gender theory and in campaigns that arise from and inform such approaches reflects as well as influences the obsessions of contemporary Western societies with sex and sexuality. Sometimes the two are difficult to disentangle. Are gender theorists and activists interested in sexuality because of the centrality of sex and sexuality in contemporary culture or are they also instrumental in putting sexuality onto the agenda? Gay rights movements and the women's movement have contributed to an understanding of how sexuality and gender are linked and have put sexuality onto the policy agenda as well as onto the curriculum of the academy.

This chapter has demonstrated a complicated and uneven process of social change in relation to thinking about gender. There are powerful continuities, for example in religious belief systems, which nonetheless have to coexist with different gender discourses. As was shown in the case of the Roman Catholic Church, whatever the certainties of faith, they still have to be defended in the public arena in ways that were not evident in earlier more traditional societies, or even, in more recent times, in the 20th century.

This also raises questions about the distinctions between stated belief and policy, on the one hand, and practice, on the other. Not only are there gaps between policies and the responses of government to social change, but there are also inconsistencies and there can be a time lapse between the policies and how they are implemented. The concept of 'gender' and theories that unpack what gender means, especially how gender identities are lived and enacted, contribute a great deal to an understanding of how inequalities are played out.

Postmodernist theories have pointed to the complexities of gender and directed attention to the importance of sexuality in debates about inequality. They have the advantage of encompassing masculinities and a more diverse range of gender identities than, for example, second-wave feminism did. However, such complex theoretical approaches run the risk of both overcomplicating the analysis of power and of prioritising personal life and intimacies through sexuality at the expense of deeply embedded economic and social inequalities that are located more obviously in the public arena. There is a danger that the approach itself will become marginal if its major concerns are with the periphery and not the centre. This chapter has argued that gender remains central to analyses of social inequality and that developments in thinking about gender can be useful and productive in exploring social and cultural change. It is necessary, however, to hold onto an understanding of both the detail of how gender is reproduced in everyday life and the unequal power relations that underpin gender differences.

6

conclusion

A major concern of this book has been to raise issues and to suggest relevant questions. Knowing which questions to ask is an important skill in the social sciences. It is only possible to know which questions to ask if you have some of the language to use in order to frame those questions.

Three of the key questions that this book has addressed are questions that are also the bases of critical analysis of social worlds and social change.

What do we mean by gender? How is gender made and remade? What are the implications of gender for policy and practice?

Definitions of 'gender' demonstrate the different dimensions of the concept as both a classification of social relations and as a theoretical concept that offers an explanation of how these social relations work. The points below summarise some of the main features of gender that have been discussed in this book. Gender is a bit more complicated than might at first appear!

- Gender is linked to sex and includes ways of classifying people as female or male.
- Sex and gender are connected, whether you see sex as a biological category and gender as a cultural and social construct, or both sex and gender as having social interrelationships.

- The term 'gender' is often preferred because gender is a more general and socially inflected way of providing description, classification and explanation.
- Gender is not a fixed category; it can be configured in different ways at different times and in different places. It can change and be changed.
- Gender and sexuality are connected but not interchangeable.
- Gender relations are underpinned by the operation of power, which has been attributed to patriarchy as an explanation of the differential power accorded to men over women in unequal social practices and institutions. Thus, gender and politics are inextricably connected.

This book has demonstrated a wide range of examples of the diverse ways in which gender differences are played out in different ways in the contemporary world by also showing how some inequalities endure into social life in the 21st century. It is the inequalities as well as the persistence of gender as a marker of difference that demand explanation and understanding of this aspect of social and political life. Empirical evidence shows the embedded binary of female and male to be the dominant model of gender, although there has been a blurring of gender boundaries in some aspects of social and cultural life and in the theorising of gender.

Does gender still matter?

Gender matters as a source of personal and collective identity. To return to the example in the Introduction to this book about the birth of a baby, albeit a fictional one in a television situation comedy, it matters whether the baby is a boy or a girl. It not only matters because the parents of the child may particularly want a girl or a boy. It also matters because gender is central to our sense of who we are. Gender is not only one of the first things you notice about a person, gender also provides each of us with a sense of self and of how each of us relates to others in the society in which we live. Gender has its own pronoun. The baby is 'he' or 'she' and is no longer 'it' once we have the knowledge of the child's gender. I have just been told the gender of the child who is to be my first grandchild. This news is not only exciting, it is also intensely emotional. I am, as they say in football, over the moon. It would not matter which gender the as-yet unborn baby was. He is a little person and has an identity and a persona. Gender is the basis of the best of human relationships; those in which we have the most personal investment and in which we experience the greatest intensities. Social and political commentators and cultural critics, however, tend to stress the more negative aspects of gender relations.

Gender also continues to matter because the evidence that is organised on the basis of gender demonstrates structural inequalities between women and men. The persistence of gender inequalities makes gender particularly important to activists and to policy makers. In the experience of gendered differences there has been an enormous resilience of the operation of patriarchal systems of power across the globe. It remains the case that the vast majority of world political leaders, leaders of industry and commerce, military leaders, heads of the judiciary and highly paid sports stars are men. Most of the wealthy and powerful people in the world are men. Women's average incomes worldwide are barely above half of men's and, in the poorest countries, especially where many women are excluded from the benefits of education and training, they are well below. The men with wealth are likely to be the same people who exercise control over others and who have more power in the exercise of world commerce and politics, the enforcement of policing and justice and, of course, warfare. Violence is more likely to be perpetrated by men, whether in the home or on the international stage of military conflict. Women and children may be among those most likely to suffer the effects of violence, including military action, but have least control of the decision-making processes that instigate it. Women have the greatest responsibility for domestic labour such as cleaning, whether in the home or in the workplace, and women do most of the childcare, even if there is more joint participation, which is recognised by neoliberal regimes that provide parental leave for those who are in paid work. When women in the UK do overcome barriers and do well, for example by becoming high achievers in education, there is great public concern about the underachievement of young men. When young women underachieved in mathematics, science and technology in the 1950s and 1960s, there was no such media furore, calling for extra classes in these subjects for girls or more places at selective schools such as grammar schools; rather an acceptance that boys do better.

Transformations are, however, taking place through the acknowledgement that gender differences and patriarchal constructions of masculinity and femininity can underpin inequalities and injustice and gender has been put onto the agenda in creative and productive ways that challenge the rigidity of entrenched boundaries and the fluidity of gender as well as the politics of difference. It is, however, by putting gender onto the agenda and by embracing a strategic politics of difference that transformations are made possible. Gender informs much of what we do in our everyday lives. It also has political importance for the following reasons:

- Gender is an important structure that shapes relations and provides the basis for the organisation of society.
- Gender matters to people as individuals in the intimate and personal relationships, to families and kinship groups, in friendship and community networks as well as to governments, policy makers and regulatory bodies.
- The persistence of gender inequalities demand both explanation and redress.

Gender and activism

The exploration of some of the key concepts in gender studies also shows the links between gender as the subject of study and gender as a category that can be investigated and described, on the one hand, and the politics and activism that have resulted from studies of gender, on the other. If you study gender and use gender as a social structure that shapes social relations, you find out that there is a great deal of gender inequality across the globe, even in those neoliberal democratic regimes that have legislation in place to combat inequalities and social exclusion. Noting inequality leads to the activism that seeks to redress inequities and establish social justice. Thus, gender as an empirical concept that provides a social structure is linked to feminism and women's political campaigns as the key organisations that arise from a study of gender. Gender is empirical in that it describes the world, theoretical in that gender provides a conceptual way of explaining social divisions, for example through the idea of patriarchy, and political in that it leads to activist campaigns such as the women's movement, which has sought to bring about greater equality both between women and men and among women. It is, however, worth making clear that gender and feminism are not the same thing and it is quite possible to study gender, to use gender as an empirical category and to measure how gender influences societies without making a commitment to feminism. It is just that feminists have been most proactive in putting gender onto the agenda.

This book has covered some of the feminist contributions in more detail because feminism incorporates theoretical critiques and programmes of intervention, many of which have been taken up by policy makers. The care of children and organisation of domestic life has been the focus of state intervention for a long time and, as feminists have demonstrated, the governance of sexual relationships and reproduction and childcare have often been informed by unstated but entrenched patriarchal principles.

Equality legislation has proliferated in neoliberal democracies although the extent of its effectiveness has been disputed. The governance of diversity and the rise of diversity politics is nonetheless testament to the impact of civil rights, feminist politics and social movements. Although they play a big part, it is not only global market forces, labour force transformations and demographic change that have led to the increased numbers of women in the labour market. Gender and an understanding of what gender means has implicatins for policy for the following reasons:

- An understanding of gender combines theory and practice.
- A study of gender provides some strategies for managing change.
- Activism has made private troubles public and shown how the personal is political.

■ Understanding gender provides a way of deconstructing apparently gender-neutral categories such as citizenship.

Sex and gender: bodies and culture

This book has suggested that gender is shaped by a whole range of factors. Biological factors play an important part as do the bodies that we inhabit. There is the form of the body a person has, its genetic make-up and anatomy and the myriad ways in which that body is the target of social, cultural and medical interventions as well as being an aspect of how a person presents themselves in the world. Bodies interact with and are acted upon by the social world. Bodies are also personal projects, for example as in sporting activities.

Gender studies has shown how it is impossible to entirely disentangle the different factors that make up what we call 'gender'. Some factors are more important than others at particular times and in particular places. There are moments in the lifecourse when the material body plays a key part in how gender is made up; none more so than in childbearing, birth and lactation. What gender studies reveals to be an oversimplification and a distortion is the argument that gender categories are based entirely on these particular aspects of gendered experience.

Social factors embrace a wide range of dimensions of the world we live in. Gendered lives are lived in different ways according to the availability of resources. Poverty is experienced in different ways for women than for men, as UN data show. Gender is deeply embedded in the organisation of social and political life, for example in the governing bodies of the state, of industry, of the military and of religious and cultural institutions. Even when offices are presented as gender neutral, it is often the case that these offices assume a male person who holds the office; gender is only marked when women occupy a position as in lady president. Nonetheless, once gender is put into discourse and acknowledged, the particularities of masculinity too and the experiences of men in the world can also be explored and understood in relation to other social differences.

Cultural factors shape how gender is lived through institutions such as education, the law, medicine, the media, popular culture and sport. Gender is discursively reproduced through the language, images and practices of different social worlds. This book has included a range of examples of different social worlds and discursive regimes in which gender categories are reinstated and challenged. In some of these examples, at one level, there may be some subversion of traditional approaches to gender difference, especially those dominated by patriarchal constructs. Women have a much stronger presence in the media, but as some of the critiques of the pornification of contemporary society demonstrate, this presence is constituted within the parameters of a continuing sexualisation and objectification of women. The dominance of these sexualised representations shows the intersection of different dimensions of exploitation, including gender, sexuality, generation, disability and race. Raunch culture may present as liberatory within a discourse of choice, but it reinstates a norm of youthful heterosexual availability; agency is only a possibility if you are young, heterosexual and non-disabled.

In other fields, masculinity, especially hegemonic masculinity, dominates. Men too are subject to the operation of gendered constraints. Sport is a social world that is strongly divided by gender and offers a very useful site for the exploration of how gendered practices work with gender categories. Although sport operates within a particularly rigid binary gender framework, it illustrates well some of the problems of the boundaries of this gender binary. Sport is also a field that shares many of the features of other aspects of popular culture and shows how gendered identities are enacted so that the actions that are performed themselves make masculinity of femininity, rather than simply being the effect of sex as biological category. How people live and perform their gender in the social world are constitutive of gender. Gender is a repeated interaction between embodied selves and social situations.

'Gender' as a theoretical and explanatory concept provides a route into asking the sort of questions that help you to unpack what is happening and to identify who is making the decisions and how power operates in any specific context.

glossary

Agency is action and energy that lead to activity on the part of human beings in directing the course of their own lives both individually and collectively. Agency is often addressed in relation to structure, to indicate the tension between the choice and autonomy of individuals and groups, on the one hand, and the constraints of social and natural structures mostly outside their control, on the other. Agency and structure intersect. While groups and individuals may be constrained by structures, those structures like patriarchy are also the product of human agency in many cases. In the context of gender, this can mean the extent to which people act to resist the inequalities of gender-based social systems.

Capitalism is an economic system that is organised around the investment of private capital in large-scale production in the pursuit of profit. Capitalism can also be seen as an historically specific stage of economic development, in the Marxist critique, which focused particularly on its manifestations in 19th-century England, as the exploitative economic system, whereby labour, as a commodity, produced profit for the bourgeoisie, the owners of the means of production, which followed feudalism. Feminists have stressed the importance of capitalism in shaping gender relations through the separation of public and private spheres in the processes of production, thus devaluing women's role in the private domestic sphere as outside the mainstream of production.

Citizenship debates have often been framed by T.H. Marshall's (1964) definition of the civil, political and social aspects of citizenship, which

---

has proved a fruitful starting point for discussion. Citizenship is not simply a legal category of person, although rights in law are crucial to the role. Feminist and gender studies have shown how the citizen has been assumed to be gender neutral but has nonetheless taken the white, middle-class man as the norm. A focus on gender demonstrates the diversity of citizenship and the importance of cultural rights in a globalised, more fluid world characterised by diasporic mobilities, technological and ecological change and cosmopolitanism.

Class is a large grouping of people who share common economic interests, experiences and lifestyles. This aspect of social divisions is linked to the economic and social organisation of any society. Some social scientists give greater emphasis to the economic organisation of production, especially in relation to ownership of the means of production or relegation to selling one's labour for a wage (Karl Marx). Others stress the importance of market position, that is, occupation, and the status that might be associated with different aspects of market position (Max Weber). Whatever the definition employed, class remains an important feature of social inequality. It is an issue that shapes social divisions in conjunction with other structures, such as gender, race and ethnicity with which class is deeply implicated.

Diaspora is the dispersal of people across the globe, originally associated with the movement of Jewish people, but now used for a diverse range of people. Diaspora has particular meanings when linked to gender and can be used to accommodate the mobilities of women in globalised economies. Diaspora is used as a category of identity, seen as particularly useful at a time of large-scale migration and to provide a means of explaining globalised identities and identities that cannot be traced to a single origin or home and incorporate often multiple sites of belonging. Diaspora is a concept used to understand globalised identities and citizenship, which cross the boundaries of the nation state, across the globe, and provides points of connection between women and men as well as disjunctions where women's experiences of migration are different from men's.

Difference is a relational concept, whereby something, or one group of people, is defined in terms of how it connects to something else or to another group. Difference can be oppositional, as in the binary opposition of men/women, with its associated dualisms of strong/weak, active/passive, or it can relate to position in relation to other phenomena. For example, Tuesday comes after Monday and before Wednesday. The French philosopher Jacques Derrida (1973) developed the notion of *différance* to accommodate a more relational and less oppositional idea of difference, which has been taken up in feminist theories. Binaries, however, often involve a hierarchical opposition where one of the two is rated above the other, especially when it comes to gender. Feminists have sought to expose gendered hierarchies and to assert the strengths of women and the characteristics associated with women. They have also explored less oppositional notions of difference, which accommodate diversity but still permit a politics of difference that can claim women's rights.

Disablist/disabling societies provide a way of shifting the emphasis from the person who has a disability to the social environment, which creates impediments to active engagement and full participation in social life. For example, the person who uses a wheelchair is not disabled if there is full wheelchair access, nor is the visually impaired person who is supported by technologies that provide alternative modes of communication. This is a contested approach, however, especially in materialist embodied critiques and other challenges within disability movements. Intersectional theorists have often stressed the need to explore how aspects of disadvantage work together to create social exclusions rather than grouping people into a single category, as has often been the case in social cohesion policies.

Discourse When deployed within social science critiques of gender, the term 'discourse' is often drawn from the work of Michel Foucault (1981) to go beyond the more common everyday meaning that focuses on language. For Foucault, it includes sets of ideas, practices, ways of producing knowledge and shaping what we do and think according to that specific knowledge. Truth is measured by the discourse itself, not by some external criteria. Thus, a discourse is true if it is thought to be so. The concept is very useful for analyses of the everyday repetition of gender differences and the power of patriarchal ways of thinking and practising.

Essentialism in gender studies refers to a set of ideas which have often been seen as in opposition to social constructionism. Essentialism suggests that gender is fixed and rooted for example in biology and psychology or to immutable forces, whereas social constructionist approaches view gender as a more fluid product of the social and cultural forces that are in play in particular places and at particular times and thus can change and be changed. Essentialists argue that there are unchanging, essential underlying aspects of gender which persist through different forms of social organisation. There are elements of essentialism in the politics of gay and lesbian activists who also argue that sexual identities are part of who they are and not a cultural practice or socially constructed. Feminists who adopt essentialist approaches would argue that, for example, women's qualities should be more highly valued and in some cases make the case for a strategic essentialism which makes feminist politics and activism possible.

Ethnicity Identities may draw on markers of visible difference and of physical characteristics but are based on social features such as language, narratives, rituals and religion. Human societies are characterised by membership of ethnic groups, where ethnicity is not the same as nation and ethnicity transcends the geographical boundaries and those of nation states. Thus, an ethnic community is a group of people whose shared identity is related to culture, history and/or language but whose relationship to territory and statehood might not be encompassed by a nation. Intersectional approaches to gender include ethnicisation and racialisation in their approaches rather than adopting an additive model where each aspect of difference or exclusion is separate or added onto others.

Gaze The gaze is associated with the psychoanalytic critiques of Hollywood film in the work of Laura Mulvey, who drew on John Berger's earlier work, which in his book *Ways of seeing* (1972) suggested that looking is gendered. The power of gender underpins what and how we see people. Mulvey (1975), in her seminal essay 'Visual pleasure and narrative cinema', argued that women always see themselves and are seen, for example in films, through men's eyes. Images of women are always mediated by the power of gender and the ways in which power is masculine. This approach has been very influential in film studies and representational theory and has been used to argue for other forms of the gaze. Not only are women objectified by the gaze, there are other forms of oppression, for example through the imperial gaze, the colonial gaze, and challenges to oppression in the child's gaze, the female gaze and the democracy of the gaze.

Gender Many social scientists use the word 'gender' to describe differences based on anatomical and physical characteristics associated with sexual difference. The term 'gender' is preferred because it includes the social and cultural dimensions of difference. Gender is used to highlight the social construction of meanings about femininity and masculinity and the importance of social divisions between women and men. This focus on gender as implicated with sexual difference allows for an understanding of the social and political aspects of sex, rather than seeing sex and gender as separate and distinct.

Globalisation is a set of social, cultural, political and economic phenomena, which are subject to many different interpretations, ranging from those who see its impact as nothing new, to globalists who argue that it is a recent and very significant phenomenon that has transformed life across the world. Some read this as a positive experience while others see it as having disastrous effects on local communities and those outside the Western, especially US, mainstream. Feminists argue that the impact has largely been particularly exploitative for women, whose gender-specific experience is so often excluded or marginalised in the debates. Increasingly, globalisation is seen as contributing to global conflict. Most commentators agree that it has had some transforming impact.

Hegemonic masculinity is a concept particularly well developed in the work of R.W. Connell (1995) to explain the networks of masculinity that are formed through the exclusion of others, notably women and gay men. This is a masculinity that is formed by no femininity and not being feminine. Masculinity is a set of identities and attributes that is constructed through embodied practices, ways of acting and interacting with others, which is not restricted to those classified as men but is strongly linked to men rather than women. The dominance of hegemonic masculinity is reinforced through body practices that are aggressive but hegemonic masculinity is also performed by those who buy into its dominance without acting in this way themselves. For example, sportsmen may act out hegemonic masculinity through their performance in the field, in the ring or on the pitch, but others, such as spectators and commentators, are also part of the networks of hegemonic masculinity.

Heterosexism refers to the social and cultural practices that create the dominance of heterosexuality as the norm through social institutions such as the family, legal and cultural institutions and discourses. Judith Butler (1990, 1993) developed the idea of the *heterosexual matrix* to demonstrate the force of this normalising culture that is repeated and reproduced through myriad different practices, from the laws of the state to everyday routines and exchanges. The concept of the 'heterosexual matrix' provides a means of understanding how heterosexuality becomes normal, through a complex set of iterative practices, rather than a biological imperative.

Identification is a psychological process of association between oneself and something else, usually someone else. In the psychoanalytic work of Sigmund Freud (1975), the child identifies with the parent of the same sex and thus comes to take on the appropriate gender identity. Identification is thus a complex psychological process and not simply a matter of copying behaviour. The term has come to be used more widely, sometimes as an alternative to 'identity', because it suggests a process rather than a fixed position and thus is preferred because identification is more dynamic and complex than identity. Processes of identification are central to gender studies especially in explaining the links between the inner world of the psyche and unconscious forces and the outer social world.

Identity politics is associated with a range of social movements in the 1970s and 1980s linked to civil rights movements of the 1960s and 1970s, which challenged traditional class politics and asserted the rights of different groups of people, for example on grounds of gender, sexuality, experience of disability, race and ethnicity. The women's movement in its different forms was one such movement that demanded many of the rights, for example to have control over their own bodies, sexuality and reproductive rights, which have become embedded in civil and human rights in nation states and international bodies such as the United Nations. Identity politics used specific aspects of identity to make political claims and made what might have been seen as personal, political.

Intersectionality is an approach to a range of social divisions and identities that are interconnected but have distinctive characteristics. For example, sexuality intersects with disability and class and policy makers have to be attentive to the specific situations of, for instance, working-class people who have disabilities. The approach has had considerable influence on policy, for example on diversity legislation and in the policies and practices of local government, for instance in relation to sexuality in lesbian, gay, bisexual, transgender/sex, queer/ questioning, intersex (LGBTQI) policies.

Intersex is the term used to encompass a variety of conditions in which a person does not conform to the typical definitions of female or male. A person may appear female but have male internal organs or have mosaic genetics with a mixture of XX and XY chromosome cells. Intersex includes a wide range of conditions, which have more recently been categorised as disorders of sex development, but intersex remains largely a medicalised condition that is more likely to be seen as requiring treatment than accepted.

Mobilities is a term used to describe one of the characteristics of 21st-century social, cultural, economic and political life, which features different sorts of movement: of peoples across the globe and within nations, of the identifications that can be made in a changing cultural climate, including political affiliations and alliances, and in situations where technological changes are transforming social life. Mobilities operate in gender-specific ways; for example, women and men have different experiences of migration.

Multicultural A multicultural society is one in which civic nationalism and multi-ethnic citizenship are accompanied by public recognition, and participating citizens from a diversity of ethnic groups enjoy equal status and esteem. In recent years, it has been argued that multiculturalism has failed because there has not been a positive celebration of multi-ethnic culture and deep tensions and suspicions remain, for example in the first decade of the 21st century especially in relation to gender, where attempts to celebrate diversity in gender relations either have not been possible or have countered, for example, secular equality practices.

Neoliberalism is a form of government associated with free markets and democratic states that are based on the idea that their citizens are self-regulating rational individuals. Following the break-up of the former USSR and the demise of communist regimes in much of the world, this form of governance was seen to have become universal. Gender is a component of the extension of rights in neoliberal regimes along with minority ethnic rights, rights of sexual citizenship, age-related rights across generations and rights of disabled people. The extent to which neoliberalism permits freedom equally to all its citizens has been called into question as a result of 21st-century anxieties about terrorism and increased risks. Economic recession has also led to a lack of confidence in the operation of the free market and especially unregulated banking and investment services. The rights of citizenship and social inclusion that have been accorded by neoliberal regimes and from which women have benefited are under threat and, for example, the many women who work in low-paid sectors of employment are most vulnerable.

Objectification is the process cited in representational theory and in feminist activism to explain how, for example, women are made into objects of the male gaze and denied autonomy as active subjects. It is often linked to sexualisation and more recently pornification.

Patriarchy is a social system in which older men dominate younger men and all men have power over women. The concept of 'patriarchy' has been central to feminist theories and practice as a social and political system in which men operate as an oppressive class. Max Weber (1976) first developed a social critique that was taken up by feminists such as Sylvia Walby (1990), who argued that patriarchy was not just a description as in Weber's work but an inequitable system of interlocking structures that operated through the production process, paid work, the state, male violence, the construction of sexuality and cultural institutions. Juliet Mitchell (1974) identified four main structures, namely production, reproduction, sexuality and childcare. Patriarchy is a system of power that some have argued works with a particular economic system such as capitalism, but others have suggested that patriarchy predates capitalism and has more universal dimensions. Earlier formulations have been criticised as too simplistic, for example in postmodernist approaches.

Performativity The idea that gender is produced through repeated processes in performativity is drawn from the work of Judith Butler (1993), who most effectively challenged the sex gender binary by demonstrating how sex, far from being a solely biological given, is socially constructed through the iterative practice. Performativity is more than a performance as in the work of the sociologist Erving Goffman (1959), whose work showed that gender identities are roles enacted in everyday life.

Politics of difference In feminist theories and activism, a politics of difference is associated with holding on to the category of woman and arguing that there remain commonalities in women's experience as well as there being enormous differences among them. Such views range across radical and material feminisms to challenges to the disintegration of feminist politics and activism in some postmodernist approaches. Such feminists argue that we do not live in a post-feminist culture even in late modernity and there are still struggles to be fought on the basis of gender, for women and men and for those who do not fit neatly into either category. The preponderance of gender inequalities and the importance of gender in shaping everyone's life experience lend considerable support to the arguments put forward by a politics of difference.

Pornification/pornogrification are terms made up to explain the extent to which the objectification and sexualisation of women are dominant in contemporary Western culture. Although women may have won the right of citizenship in neoliberal democracies, third-wave and popular feminists, such as Ariel Levy (2006) and Natasha Walter (2010), have shown how women are constrained by the excessive stress on their sexuality and physical appearance, which is not just sexual but is also exploitative in the power that such discursive regimes exercise. So great is this power that young women are compelled to buy into male fantasies of subordination, for example by attending a work trip to a lap dancing club and passing off its pornographic aspects as ironic.

Postmodernism This school of thought refers to a set of theories that challenge modernism and the existence of universals and grand theories that purport to explain all aspects of social life. It counters the all-embracing approaches of the 'grand theories' such as Marxism, by suggesting that there is no single organising framework of society, which is diverse and segmented. Such theories are attractive to gender theorists because they often focus on representation and culture and the myriad different ways in which meanings about gender are produced, and the fragmentation of contemporary societies, in which different forms of power operate and gender articulates with other social divisions such as race, ethnicity, class, disability and generation. Postmodernism has, nonetheless, been criticised for being itself a meta theory and, at times, too complex in its attempts to engage with the fragmentation of contemporary social worlds.

Power The concept of 'power' is central to an understanding of gender, partly through ideas about men as a dominant class that exercises power and control over women at various sites, such as the family and in the public arena of paid work and offices of the state. There has been a bureaucratisation of power that operates through institutions. Power can thus be seen as operating hierarchically from the top down or, on the other hand, as more diffuse and present in all human exchanges.

This view has had considerable purchase in gender studies because, as presented by Michel Foucault(1981), it claims that power is not only diffuse, but productive as well as illustrating constraint and even coercion. Power can be the power to do something as well as involving someone having the power to stop you doing something. Change is possible through resistance to existing regimes of power. However, as feminists have pointed out, when power is everywhere it is difficult to locate the source of power, for example in patriarchal systems.

Queer theory is a postmodernist set of ideas most strongly linked to the work of Judith Butler (1993). Such an approach arises out of post-structuralist and postmodernist challenges to the grand theories of sociology such as those of Karl Marx, who posited a meta theory to explain human societies and historical change. Postmodernism challenges the primacy of the economic structure of society and queer theory takes up the uncertainties and fluidity of these ways of thinking and focuses on sexuality as a site for diversity and contingency. Butler explored the possibilities of crossing traditional boundaries and understanding social forces through an understanding of those who do not conform. Queer theory subverts norms and expectations.

Race The term 'race' permits social scientists to stress the political significance of race and ethnicity and the use of 'race' in inverted commas shows that race is not a fixed biological category, but a dynamic, changing social concept. Race is not now used in the social sciences to describe biological make-up but the term is retained in order to hold onto the historical and political dimensions of this aspect of difference. Race, more than the term 'ethnicity', allows for recognition of racism and racist practices that discriminate against people of different ethnicities.

Reproduction refers to the reproduction of the species and to the reproduction of gender roles through the patriarchal systems that operate in relation to producing the next generation of people. Reproduction is of people and values. Feminists stress how the meta theories of modernism, such as Marxism, emphasised the importance of production in the economy as shaping social relations and social organisation but failed to accommodate reproduction and in particular the gendered roles that are implicated in this and how they are organised, for example within families and households.

Roles The society into which we are born presents us with a series of roles, which are rather like parts in a play. The scripts are mostly already written, although, depending on our social and economic position and individual attributes, we can interpret these roles in different ways. A role comes with a pattern of behaviour, routines and responses. Although not the same as identities, roles offer a useful description of the social component of an identity. Development of theories about the significance of roles is associated with the work of Erving Goffman (1959).

Sex/gender The sex/gender binary is very important in gender studies, especially in the questioning of assumptions about the fixity of biology. Theories and practices have moved from simple assumptions about sex and gender as biologically determined and fixed, through an exploration of how gender is socially constructed, to a reappraisal of sex and more detailed discussion of the ways in which sex too has social meanings and sex is affected by and affects gender relations in the wider society.

Sexualisation refers to dominant modes of representing women in particular. For example, women's visible presence in the media is often accompanied by commentary on their physical appearance as attractive (or not). Women's sexual attractiveness or lack of it has primacy in their public presence that is largely not accorded to men who are permitted to just 'be', for example an athlete or a politician. Women are mothers or grandmothers or WAGs (wives and girlfriends of athletes), good looking or plain. Female athletes may be described as masculine. Women always have to negotiate these sexualising identities while heterosexual men mostly do not have to, unless they choose to.

Social exclusion Some groups are marginalised and cut off from full participation in social, political, economic and cultural life. These groups are not able to take full advantage of all that is available in these areas to the more affluent members of society. Social exclusion has been the target of neoliberal governments, which have sought to promote greater social inclusion and cohesion, through policies that have increasingly been called 'diversity policies'. Many of the policy initiatives that have targeted social exclusion within neoliberal governance associate gender with women. For example, women have been included as a homogeneous group in the target communities that embrace many aspects of social exclusion such as race, ethnicity, disability, class, disaffection, deviance or criminal behaviour.

Structure is used, often in conjunction with agency, to describe some of the organised or systematic, coherent constraints on human activity. Structures may take the form of social institutions, for example those of the state, or discourses that organise ideas and practices, such as those of gender and ethnicity, or be based in physical or biological, embodied dimensions of experience. Structures are created and shaped by human agency in different ways, at different times and in different contexts.

Symbolising involves making one word, object or image stand for another. For example, a green traffic light means that you can proceed and a red traffic light means that you have to stop. The notion of symbolising is used extensively in gender studies as part of systems of representation through which we make sense of gender identities. The media play a key role in promoting gender identifications and categories, which are often stereotypical, as in the highly sexualised images of women, which also marginalise those who do not conform, for example, to particular body types.

The state is a grouping of institutions that claim ultimate law-making authority over a particular territory. The state will also claim the monopoly on legitimate use of violence and coercion. The state is a key location for the exercise of patriarchal power and managing institutions through which gender is made and remade and becomes embedded in social practices as well as in the law. For example, the state regulates sexual behaviour, family organisation and responsibilities. Many social scientists use the term 'governance' to cover the activities of the state and the term 'governmentality' to embrace a wider set of legal and quasi-legal interventions through which social life is regulated and citizens are produced.

Transgender covers a range of identities and practices that vary from conventional gender roles. Transgender embraces a diversity of sexual identifications and usually involves an understanding of the self that does not fit with the gender assigned at birth. Transgender includes ambiguities and increasingly 'trans' is used to cover a range of identities that incorporate transgender and transsexuality and thus include a diverse and fluid range. Trans connotes transgression of norms and challenges traditional values.

Transsexuality, like transgender, involves a failure of identification with the sex/gender ascribed at birth but transsexual people are more likely to identify with the opposite sex and may choose to undergo medical treatment such as surgery to enable them to move into what they perceive as their true sex/gender.

Unconscious The 'unconscious' is a concept strongly associated with psychoanalytic thought and especially the work of Sigmund Freud (1975). The unconscious mind is that part of the mind into which all the desires and feelings that we have had to suppress are deposited. For example, when a small child's needs are not met they repress these feelings into the unconscious. These feelings can emerge, often unexpectedly later in life, for example in dreams, in jokes or in slips of the tongue. Thus, dreams can be significant in revealing the feelings we have of which we are not otherwise conscious.

references

Beechey, V. (1979) 'On patriarchy', *Feminist Review*, vol 3, pp 66-82.

Bem, S. L. (1976) 'Sex typing and androgyny: Further explorations of the expressive domain', *Journal of personality and social psychology*, vol 34, p 1016.

Berger, J. (1972) *Ways of seeing*, London: Penguin.

Bhavnani, K. and Coulson, M. (1986) 'Transforming socialist feminism: the challenge of racism', *Feminist Review*, vol 23, pp 81-92.

Birke, L. (1986) *Women, feminism and biology: The feminist challenge*, New York, NY: Methuen Press.

Blade Runner (1982) dir Ridley Scott, Warner Brothers.

Bourdieu, P. (1984) *Distinction. A social critique of the judgement of taste*, trans. R. Nice, Cambridge, MA: University of California Press.

Butler, J. (1990) *Gender trouble: Feminism and the subversion of identity*, London: Routledge.

Butler, J. (1993) *Bodies that matter: On the discursive limits of sex*, London: Routledge.

Carby, H. (1987) *Reconstructing womanhood: The emergence of the Afro-American woman novelist*, Oxford: Oxford University Press.

Cixous, H. (1980) 'Sorties' in E. Marks and I. Courtviron (eds.) *New French feminisms: An anthology*, Amherst, MA: University of Massachusetts Press.

Collins, P.H. (2000) *Black feminist thought: Knowledge, consciousness and the politics of empowerment*, New York, NY: Routledge.

Connell, R.W. (1995) *Masculinities,* Cambridge: Polity.

Connell, R.W. (2009) *Gender* (2nd edition), Cambridge: Polity Press.

Daly, M. (1978) *Gyn/ecology: The metaethics of radical feminism*, Boston, MA: Beacon Press.

DCMS (Department For Culture, Media And Sport) (1999) *Policy Action Team 10: A report to the Social Exclusion Unit – arts and sport*, London: DCMS.

DCMS and SU (Strategy Unit) (2002) *Game plan: A strategy for delivering government's sport and physical activity objectives*, London: Cabinet Office.

De Beauvoir, S. (1989 [1949]) *The second sex*, trans. H. Parshley, New York: Vintage Books.

Delphy, C. (1996) 'Rethinking sex and gender', trans. D. Leonard, in L. Adkins and D. Leonard (eds.) *Sex in question: French materialist feminism*, London: Taylor and Francis.

Derrida, J. (1973) *'Speech and phenomena' and other essays on Husserl's theory of signs*, trans. D. B. Allison, Evanston: Northwestern University Press.

Durkheim, E. (1952) *Suicide a study in sociology*, London: Routledge.

Engels, F. (1972) *The origins of the family, private property and the state, in the light of the researches of Lewis H. Morgan*, New York, NY: International Publishers.

FAO (Food and Agriculture Organization) (2011) 'Food and agricultural organisation of the United Nations', www.fao.org/kids/en/equalrights.html

Fausto-Sterling, A. (2005) 'Bare bones of sex: part II', *Signs*, vol 30, no 2, pp 1491-528.

Firestone, S. (1970) *The dialectic of sex. The case for feminist revolution*, London: Jonathan Cape.

Foucault, M. (1981) *The history of sexuality: Volume 1: An introduction*, Harmondsworth: Penguin.

Freud, S. (1975) *The psychopathology of everyday life*, Harmondsworth: Penguin.

Goffman, E. (1959) *The Presentation of self in everyday life*, New York: Doubleday.

Gutiérrez-Rodriguez, E. (2010) *Migration, domestic work and affect*, London: Routledge.

Haraway, D. (1991) *Simions, cyborgs and women: the reinvention of nature*, London: Free Association Books.

Hartman, H. (1981) 'The unhappy marriage of Marxism and feminism: towards a more progressive union', in Sargent (ed) *Women and revolution*, London: Pluto.

Hochschild, A. (1983) *The managed heart: The commercialization of human feeling*, Berkeley, CA: University of California Press. Reprinted 2003.

ILO (International Labour Organization) (2011) 'ILO Participatory gender audit', www.fao.org/Participation/ft_show.jsp?ID=6823

ILO Wage Gap (2009) 'Global wage report: 2009 update', www.ilo.org/global/resources/WCMS_116500/lang--en/index.htm

Irigaray, L. (1985) *This sex which is not one,* New York: Cornell University Press.

Kristof, N. and WuDunn, S. (2010) *Half the sky: How to change the world*, London: Virago.

Lacan, J. (1977) *Ecrits: A selection*, London: Tavistock.

Levy, A. (2005) *Female chauvinist pigs: Women and the rise of raunch culture*, New York, NY: Free Press.

Lloyd, M. (2007) *Judith Butler*, Cambridge: Polity.

Mead, G.H. (1934) *Mind, self and society*, Chicago IL: University of Chicago Press.

Marshall, T.H. (1964) 'Citizenship and class', in B.S. Turner and P. Hamilton (eds) *Citizenship: Critical concepts* (vol 2), London: Routledge, pp 5-44.

Marx, K. and Engels, F. (1968) *Selected works in one volume*, London: Lawrence and Wishart.

Mead, M. (1950) *Male and female: The classic study of the sexes*, London: HarperCollins.

Miller, D. and Woodward, S. (2010) *Global denim*, London: Berg.

Mitchell, J. (1974) *Psychoanalysis and feminism*, Freud, Reich, Laing and Women, Harmondsworth: Penguin.

Mohanty, C.T. (1988) 'Under Western eyes: feminist scholarship and colonial discourses', Feminist Review, no 30 (Autumn), pp 61-88.

Mohanty, C.T. (2003) *Feminism without borders: Decolonizing theory*, Practicing Solidarity Durham: Duke University Press.

Morgan, R. (1970) *Sisterhood is powerful: An anthology of writings from the women's liberation movement*, New York: Random House.

Morgan, R. (1984) *Sisterhood is global*, New York: The Feminist Press.

Mulvey, L. (1975) 'Visual pleasure and narrative cinema', *Screen*, vol 16, no 3, pp 6-18.

Oakley, A. (1972) *Sex, gender and society*, London: Temple Smith.

Oakley, A. (1981) *Subject woman*, Harmondsworth: Penguin.

Pateman, C. (1988) *The sexual contract*, Cambridge: Polity.

Parekh, B. (2000) *The future of multi ethnic Britain. The Parekh report*, London: Profile Books.

Phillips, A. (1987) *Divided loyalties: Dilemmas of sex and class*, London: Virago.

Richardson, D. and Robinson V. (eds) (2007) *Introducing gender and women's studies* (3rd edition), Basingstoke: Palgrave.

Royal College of Nursing (2010) 'Mixed-sex accommodation has no place in 21st century health care' www.rcn.org.uk/newsevents/news/article/uk/mixed-sex_accommodation_has_no_place_in_21st_century_health_care

Rubin, G. (1975) 'The traffic in women: notes on the "political economy" of sex', in Rayna Reiter (ed) *Toward an anthropology of women*, New York: Monthly Review Press, pp 790-4.

Spivak, G.C (1988) 'Can the subaltern speak?' in C. Nelson and L. Grossberg (eds) *Marxism and the interpretation of culture*, Urbana/Chicago: University of Illinois Press, pp 271-313.

UN Decade of Women (1975 & 1985) 'Global issues: Women', see www.un.org/en/globalissues/women/

Walby S. (1990) *Theorizing patriarchy*, Oxford: Basil Blackwell.

Walter, N. (2010) *Living dolls: The return of sexism*, London: Virago.

Ware, V. (1992) *Beyond the pale: White women, racism and history*, London: Verso.

Weber, M. (1976 [1905]) *The protestant ethic and the rise of capitalism*, London: Allen and Unwin.

Woodward, K. (1997) *Identity and difference*, London: Sage Publications.

Woodward, K. (2007) *Boxing masculinity and identity. The 'I' of the tiger*, London: Routledge.

Woodward, K. (2009a) *Social sciences: The big issues*, London: Routledge.

Woodward, K. (2009b) *Embodied sporting practices: regulating and regulatory bodies*, Basingstoke: Palgrave.

Woodward, K. and Woodward, S. (2009) *Why feminism matters: Feminism lost and found*, Basingstoke: Palgrave Macmillan.

Woodward, S. (2007) *Why women wear what they wear*, London: Berg.

Young, I.M. (2005) *Female body experiences: Throwing like a girl and other essays on feminist philosophy and social theory*, Oxford: Oxford University Press.

Index

A

abortion 95
advertising 72
age 102
  ageing 60, 75
  ageism 59
agency 115
aggression 67
Anglican Church 93
anthropology 12–13
  anthropological evidence 12, 23
archaeologists 66
Archbishop of Canterbury 94

B

baby/babies 9–10, 108–9
Beattie, T. (Lagondino, T.) 26, 30, 38
Beijing Olympics 76–7
Berger, J. 118
biology xi, 4, 11, 13, 17, 25, 36–7, 43, 57, 62,
  66, 80, 112, 126
  biological classifications 1, 13, 39
Birke, L. 17
bodies 25, 65–7, 68, 71, 84–5, 112
  and culture 79
  enfleshed characteristics xii, 3,
body practices 33, 68
Bourdieu, P. x
boxing 30
Butler, J. 18, 23, 33, 57, 91, 100, 120

C

capitalism 15–16, 115
  capitalist labour market 45
Cardinal John Henry Newman 94, 96
Chen-Oster, C. 99
cheetah blades 77
children
  childbirth 66, 108
  child bearing and rearing 49, 79–81, 109,
    111
  child abuse 95–6
Christian Right 58
citizenship 47–8, 50, 53, 56, 62, 115
civil partnerships 10, 58–9, 102
  Civil Partnership Act (2004) 58
civil society 49
civil rights 45, 48, 111
Cixous, H. 14
class xii, 2, 14, 23, 42, 47, 92, 116
coalition government (2010) 60
Collins, P.H. 101
Commonwealth Games 78
connection 62

Connell R. 91, 119
continuities 88
  and change 90, 93
contraception 46
cultural
  change 47
  constructions 61
  identities 36
  practices 3, 113
cyborgs 75–6, 90, 92

D

Daly, M. 14
de Beauvoir, S. 5, 12
Delphy, C. 15
demographic change 11, 49
denim 65
Derrida, J. 117
diaspora 116
  diasporic mobilities 62
difference 51, 104, 107
disability xii, 14, 76, 78, 92, 102, 113, 117
  disablist prejudice 52
disadvantaged groups 55
discourse 117
discrimination 60, 77, 97–101, 104–5
  discriminatory acts 59, 99
  direct sexual discrimination 103
  indirect discrimination 102
diversity policies xii, 42, 53, 55, 58, 111
DNA x, 37
domestic
  labour 23, 51, 81, 109
  violence 7, 16, 45–6, 92
dressing 74–5
Durkheim, E. 11

E

economic systems 66, 71
education 10
embodiment 68
  embodied characteristics x, 43, 57, 70
  embodied differences 67
employment patterns 11
empowerment 74–5
Engels, F. 11
environment 66
equality
  and difference xii, 50, 52–3
  Equality Act (2010) 53–4, 88, 101–2
  equality legislation 44, 91, 100–1, 111
  equal pay 46, 103
  Equal Pay Acts (1970 and 1980) 54
  equal opportunities 46

equal rights xii
essentialism 22, 56, 91, 118
ethnicity xii, 2, 14, 42, 45, 92, 118
European Union Directives 54

F

families/family life 45, 50, 57, 60, 82–3, 92, 110
  nuclear family 82
Food and Agriculture Organization (FAO) 5
fathers 49
Fausto-Sterling, A. 66
female
  bodies 66
  female/male dichotomy 1, 5, 18, 23, 28, 30, 43, 59
feminists 69, 72, 82
  feminisms xi, 90
  anti-porn activism 73
  campaigns 52, 88
  critiques xii, 12
  post-colonial studies 62
  theorists and activists 1, 11, 20, 82–3, 88, 90, 91–2
femininity 13, 35, 44, 62, 113, 119
fertility 17
Firestone, S. 90
fluidity of categories and concepts xii, 4, 19, 41, 57, 88, 108, 110
football 30
  Football Association (FA) 8, 30
Foucault, M. 35, 53, 70–1, 97, 105, 117
Freudian psychoanalysis 12, 70, 120, 128

G

gay and lesbian rights 45, 88, 95, 105
gaze 118
gender *passim*
  and age 60
  and sexuality 56–9, 73
  as a classificatory tool 5, 104, 107
  as social structure 41, 111
  categories 2, 18, 39, 41, 62, 70, 77, 88, 104, 110, 112–13
  definitions 3–5, 14, 104, 107, 110–11
  democracy xii
  difference x, 1, 4–5, 25, 62, 67, 108
  frameworks 3
  identities ix, 3, 34, 43–4, 62, 71–3, 106, 113
  inequalities 5, 12, 20, 23, 42, 50–1, 104
  key questions xi
  politics 47
gender reassignment 102
  Gender Reassignment Act (2003) 54
gender relations 1–3, 15, 107
gender studies xi, xiii, 1, 3, 11, 47, 62, 90–1, 110
gender theorists 105
gender verification 31–7

gendered body/bodies xii, 65, 67–8, 71, 84–5
  practices 10, 67, 84, 113
  representations xii
  ungendered 2
generation xii, 56, 92, 113
genital mutilation 7
global economy 71, 89, 111
globalisation 17, 43, 88, 116, 119
girls and education 6
Goffman, E 33, 126
grandchild 109

H

harassment 102
Haraway, D. 75, 92
hegemonic masculinity 77, 91, 100, 113, 119
heterosexuality 23, 35, 72, 82–3, 91, 113
  heterosexism 24
  heterosexual matrix 19, 24, 120
  heterosexual family setup 49
  heterosexual relations 57
hierarchical division 4, 13
HIV / AIDS 7
homophobia 35, 57, 75, 91
human rights 48
human societies 3

I

identification 120
identity politics 16, 121
Iliescu, A. 80, 83
inequality: and difference xiii, 106, 108–9
  global inequalities xii, 8–9, 110
International Association of Athletics Federations (IAAF) 31, 34, 77, 79
International Labour Organization 6
International Olympic Committee (IOC) 8
internet 75, 90, 92
intersectionality 101, 103, 121
intersex x, 37, 43
interventions 58, 81
Irigaray, L. 14
Islam 51, 94
issues of clothing 51
IVF 70, 80, 95

J

Judaism 93

K

key questions 107

L

labour market 88, 100
Labour Party 60
Lacanian psychoanalysis 14, 16
language and gender 2, 3, 14
legal barriers 50
legal processes 29

legislation: anti-discriminatory xii, 58
Levy, Ariel 73
LGBTQI label 58, 91, 121
life expectancy 10

M

male
  aggression 46
  dominance 14, 16
  gaze 69, 72, 122
  male–female binary xii, 3, 15, 38
Malinowski, B. 12
marriage 10–11, 58–9, 102
Marshall, T.H. 48, 115
Marx, K. 11
  Marxist critique 115, 125
masculinity 13–14, 19, 33, 35–6, 44, 47, 62,
  77, 91–2, 99–100, 106, 113, 119
materiality xii, 88
  material bodies 67-8, 112
Mead, M. 12
media 33, 61, 69, 71–2, 78, 84, 96, 113
medical science 35
  medicine 70
men 3, 109
menopause 80
misogyny 45
Mitchell, J. 16, 123
mixed-sex wards 60–1
Mohanty, C. 17–18
monogamous coupledom 58
Morgan, R. 17
mother 70
  mother–daughter relationship 14
  motherhood xi, 70, 84
multiculturalism 51, 122
Mulvey, L. 118

N

nature 27
neoliberalism 49, 122
  neoliberal democracies 50, 81, 100
  neoliberal economies 71
  neoliberal governance 91
  neoliberal interventions 54
  neoliberal regimes 51, 109–10, 122

O

Oakley, Ann 13, 21
Oedipus complex 12
objectification 74, 113, 122
older women 61, 80–3
Olympic Games 32, 36
ordination of women priests 96

P

paid work 42
Paralympics (2008) 76, 78
Parekh Report 51
parenthood xi
patriarchal culture 12, 109–10, 113

patriarchy 4, 12, 15, 17, 23, 45, 49, 57–8, 77,
  81–2, 100, 104, 107, 111, 123
pension funds 60
performativity 18, 24, 125
personal life 42
physical appearance 65
Pistorius, O. ('Blade-Runner') 76–9
policy making and practice xi, 1
politics of difference 14, 123
Pope Benedict XVI, visit to Britain (2010)
  94–5
popular culture xii, 71–4, 113
pornification (pornogrification) 69, 73–4,
  85, 113
pornography 69, 73-4
post-apartheid South Africa 78
post-colonialism 90–1
postfeminism 88
postgender 87–8
post-menopausal women 80, 83
postmodernist approaches
poverty 112
power 16, 103–6, 107, 118
power relations 2, 36
primary legislation on equality 53
prisons 70
professional bodies 70
psychoanalysis 16, 120
  psychoanalytic views 14
psychological characteristics 67
psychology and psychologists 11, 34, 89

Q

Queen of England 94–5
queer studies 47, 89
queer theory 11, 23–4, 57, 91

R

race xii, 42, 45, 92, 102, 113, 125
racism 75
rape 7
regulatory framework 36
religion 51, 92–3 97, 102, 105
religious intolerance 93
representation of women 69, 74, 84
representing bodies 68, 71
reproduction xi, 3, 7, 10, 11, 25, 38, 46
reproductive technologies xi, 70, 81, 83
roles 126
Roman Catholic Church 93, 96, 105
Royal College of Nursing 61
Rubin, G. 13

S

same-sex relationships 58–9, 95
secondary bodily characteristics 29
second-wave feminism 11–12, 17, 90, 106
secrecy clauses 103
self 74
Semenya, C. 31, 33–7, 70, 77, 79
sex x, xii, 19, 24, 102–3, 105

sex and gender Chapter Two *passim*, 41, 81, 112
sex and gender connections xi, 101, 105, 107
sex and gender differences 13, 17, 22, 24, 37, 126
sex discrimination 30, 52
Sex Discrimination Act (1975) 54
sex–gender divide x, 13, 18, 23, 38, 43–4
sexual citizenship 56
   sexual orientation 102
sexualisation 69, 126
sexualised images 69
sexuality xii, 2, 4, 16, 42, 44, 91–2, 105
   sexuality and gender 54, 96–7
single-sex wards 61
social
   change 105–6, 107
   construction 4, 22, 30, 33, 57, 62
   context 66, 88
   differences 113
   exclusion 51, 59, 62, 103, 126
   forces 56, 60, 66, 70, 85
   justice 48, 82
   mother 70
   movements 45, 111
   practices 4, 107
   processes 20
   psychologists 23
   relations xi, 9, 44, 62, 104, 110
   sciences 89
   systems 12, 15
   values 23
socialisation of children 22, 38
Spivac, G.C. 18, 91
sport 30, 36–7, 67-8, 70, 76, 113
   and society 34
   sporting practices 33–4
   sports medicine 67
   sports regulatory bodies 30, 38
   sports science 18
state institutions 112, 127
stereotypes 34–5
Stoller, R. 13
structure 127
students 10
suffrage 12, 50
surrogate mother 80
symbolising processes 69, 127

T

technology 75–6, 90, 116
technoscience 76, 79, 80, 82–3
Thatcher, M. 47
third-wave feminists 69, 89
third world women 17
transformation of gender 97
transgender x, 26, 28–30, 37, 43, 128
transgression 19
transsexuality 128
Truth, S. 43

U

UK Department for Media, Culture and Sport 55
UK Social trends 9
UN data 50
UN Decade of Women 17, 47
UN Declaration of Human Rights 28
UN Human development reports 5, 7–9, 19
unconscious, the 128
unequal relationships 100
US imperialism 90

V

victimisation 103
violence 7, 109
   visualisation of women's bodies 73

W

Walby, S. 123
Weber, M. 12, 116, 123
welfare systems 48–9
whiteness 78
widening participation 54
women 68, 73, 81, 88
   and health 6
   and men xii, 4, 12, 105
   as a homogeneous group 46
   black women 102
   differences between 42–3, 46, 56
   in government 8
   in post-industrialised countries 56
   in trades unions 47
   professionals 98
   world's poor 5–6
women's
   bodies xii, 69, 72
   boxing 67
   experience 91
   liberation 15
   magazines 72
   movement 42, 45, 47, 105
   oppression 57
   rights and needs 52
   studies xi, 1, 47, 89
Woodward, K. 74, 83, 91
Woodward, S. 74, 83
workplace 52, 82, 88
World Athletics Championship 31
World Health Organization (WHO) 7
World Wide Web 75, 92

Y

Young, I.M. 68